God is an Earthquake

GOD IS AN EARTHQUAKE

The Spirituality of Margery Kempe

SANTHA BHATTACHARJI

DARTON · LONGMAN + TODD

First published 1997 by
Darton, Longman and Todd Ltd
1 Spencer Court
140–142 Wandsworth High Street
London SW18 4JJ

ISBN 0–232–52140–9

A catalogue record for this book is available from the British Library.

Designed by Roger Lightfoot

Phototypeset by Intype London Ltd
Printed and bound in Great Britain by
Redwood Books, Trowbridge, Wiltshire

IN MEMORY OF
ROSEMARY WOOLF

CONTENTS

FOREWORD xi

INTRODUCTION: Discovering Margery Kempe........xiv

1. THE NATURE OF THE EVIDENCE...................... 1

2. MARGERY'S LIFE: UNRAVELLING ITS CHRONOLOGY..... 9

3. MADNESS... 24

4. TEARS AND SCREAMING 39

5. JOURNEYS.. 51

6. TRIALS FOR HERESY.............................. 67

7. VISIONS 84

8. CONVERSATIONS WITH CHRIST 99

9. MARGERY'S TEACHING 115

CONCLUSION: Was Margery a mystic?...............133

NOTES...141

SELECT BIBLIOGRAPHY............................153

ACKNOWLEDGEMENTS

THIS BOOK grew out of a larger project originally suggested by Lesley Riddle, then Editorial Director at Darton, Longman and Todd. I am indebted to her and to all her helpers and successors at DLT for their encouragement, patience, good humour and support over a number of years, particularly to Morag Reeve, the late Sarah Baird-Smith, Mary Jean Pritchard, Jane Williams and David Moloney. I am also indebted to Sr Benedicta Ward, SLG, for encouraging me to take on this project in the first place.

All translations from *The Book of Margery Kempe* in this study are my own, as are most of the translations from other medieval texts. Where I have used the work of other translators, this is indicated in the Notes. In particular, I have used the following: Walter Hilton, *The Ladder of Perfection*, trans. Leo Sherley-Price, Penguin Classics (London, 1957); St Catherine of Siena, *The Dialogue*, trans. Suzanne Noffke, Classics of Western Spirituality (New York, 1980). I have also quoted briefly from Anthony de Mello, *Sadhana: A Way to God* (New York, 1984).

FOREWORD

'THEN HER . . . cries and weeping increased so much that priests did not dare to give her communion openly in the church, but privately, in the Prior's chapel at Lynn, out of people's hearing.'

The cryings of Margery Kempe have been the subject of much discussion and criticism both today and from the day when they began. The attempt to keep her 'out of people's hearing' has continued, whether by the physical muffling of her contemporaries, the total loss of her book until sixty years ago, or by the attempts of modern critics to psychoanalyse her into insignificance. Margery Kempe, however, was not to be kept down now or then. Indeed, in one of her sessions of 'dalliance' with Christ, he promised that this would be so: 'Then our blessed Lord said to her mind, Daughter, I will not have my grace hidden that I give you, for the busier people are to hinder it and prevent it, the more I shall spread it abroad and make it known to all the world.'

Dr Bhattacharji's work is a sustained attempt to 'make it known' by seeing Margery in her own setting, literary and historical, and in her own terms. As a result, Margery's book then seems not the work of an hysterical show-off, or of an early feminist ranged against a world of men, but as a remarkable though not unique woman of her times. In particular it liberates her central message, that of 'seeing Christ through the medium of the human beings she encounters as she goes about her normal business in the streets' (p. 172). Her 'autobiography' forms part of several distinct genres and she is discussed here as part, albeit a dramatic part, of the traditions of medieval mystics and visionaries, of travellers, and of converted sinners.

The Book of Margery Kempe, dictated by a woman of much experience recollecting forty years of her life in old age, belongs in some ways to the tradition of spiritual autobiography. The most notable exponents of this form of spiritual discourse, Augustine of Hippo in the fourth century and Peter Abelard in the twelfth, gave detailed accounts of their personal experience from youth to maturity in order to show the work of God. They, and others to a lesser degree, used the path of self knowledge, in accounts sometimes rueful, sometimes bitter, but always rooted in their later repentance where the hand of God manifest in their lives had created a true perception of themselves. *The Book of Margery Kempe*, the first autobiography in English, has not the theological sophistication of either Augustine and Abelard or of her nearer contemporary, Catherine of Siena; nor does it show their depth of self-knowledge. Absorbed with herself, the 'selective economy of her memory' (p. 96) combined with her lack of practice in literary self-expression, produced a somewhat confused account of her life in terms of 'best friends and worst enemies' (p. 46).

This is not to relegate Margery to a second-class place among the autobiography experts, but to recognise the less sophisticated nature of her 'Book'. Nor, on the other hand, can she be placed entirely within in the outré tradition of 'fools for Christ' particularly admired in Eastern Christendom. Unsophisticated but not mad, Margery is part of many categories rather than one. Dr Bhattacharji lays bare the full extent of Margery's limitations and eccentricities, and then sets her life in the practical ethos and expectations of her own times. From this she draws conclusions about the continued usefulness of the book, so that it appears providential that it should have been brought to light in the mid-twentieth century.

The Book of Margery Kempe may not be a text in the first rank of spiritual writings but it is not simply the 'reminiscences of an old lady' of the fourteenth century (p. 1). Margery is more than that; she is presented in these pages as an independent, sincere and devout woman of her times. After the earthquake of feminist examination here is the still small voice of clarity, reason and discernment.

Sister Benedicta Ward SLG

Introduction

DISCOVERING MARGERY KEMPE

NOWADAYS, WHEN anyone picks up a book on the group of medieval writers commonly known as 'the English Mystics', they will probably find in it five particular authors: Richard Rolle; the anonymous author of the *Cloud of Unknowing*; Walter Hilton; Julian of Norwich; and Margery Kempe. Before 1934, however, they would have found only the first four.

It was only in that year that a distinguished Middle English scholar, Hope Emily Allen, discovered the lost *Book of Margery Kempe*. She announced this momentous event in a long letter to *The Times* of 27 December 1934, beginning:

> Sir – It was said regretfully (not long ago) by a distinguished historian that in the Middle Ages old ladies did not write their reminiscences. The reminiscences of a medieval old lady have lately come to light in the library of Lieutenant-Colonel W. Butler-Bowdon, D.S.O. (already known as the public-spirited inheritor of several fine medieval objects, which have been exhibited at the Victoria and Albert Museum, Burlington House, and the Heralds' College). This manuscript was sent to the Victoria and Albert Museum for identification.[1]

The letter goes on to describe, in about eight hundred words, the content and significance of the book, in a way calculated to arouse the interest not just of medievalists, but of the public at large. Writing out of her vast knowledge of the period, Hope Allen's description is of an accuracy and succinctness yet to be bettered in any later study of Margery Kempe, and yet it could hardly have prepared Margery's audience for the shock in store for them.

As the letter indicates, the *Book* had been preserved in a single manuscript, dated to about 1440, in the private ownership of Colonel William Butler-Bowdon, in whose family it had been from at least the eighteenth century, and even before – 'from time immemorial'.[2] As one of the ancient Catholic families of England, the Bowdons seem to have had an interest in acquiring and preserving devotional works written before the Reformation. Indeed, many medieval religious works have come down to us through this kind of activity, carried out by private collectors from the sixteenth century onwards.[3]

Before the Dissolution of the Monasteries in 1539, this single manuscript of Margery Kempe's work had been owned, at some point, by the Carthusian monks of Mount Grace in Yorkshire.[4] In the fifteenth century, the Carthusians were great copyists and disseminators of works of spirituality, and their interest in Margery tells us something of the value placed on her in her own day.

When the manuscript was brought to the Victoria and Albert Museum, Hope Allen happened to be in London, rather than in her native America, on an academic grant to work on a thirteenth-century religious text for women, the *Ancrene Wisse.* Apparently, it was at the suggestion of the well-known writer on mysticism, Evelyn Underhill, that she was invited to the Museum to examine the manuscript. Friends later spoke of her eyes 'shining with excitement' as she described her find.[5]

The manuscript has since been deposited in the British Library.[6]

BEFORE 1934

Before the discovery of the manuscript, the name of Margery Kempe was already known to modern scholars, through a short collection of extracts 'taken out of the Book of Margery Kempe', produced as a pamphlet by the early printer Wynkyn de Worde in 1501.[7]

These extracts seem to have been sufficiently well-received at the time to be reprinted by Henry Pepwell in 1521, as the third item in a miscellany of only seven devotional texts. The other pieces consisted of four short works traditionally ascribed to the *Cloud* author, a short piece by Walter Hilton, and some extracts from the writings of St Catherine of Siena.[8]

A slightly modernised version of this miscellany, entitled *The Cell of Self-Knowledge*, was published by Edmund Gardner in 1910,[9] and it was probably this book which familiarised twentieth-century readers with the name of Margery Kempe, and caused them to look forward eagerly to reading her complete work.

The extracts, though not departing significantly from conventional medieval piety, were fresh and strong in style. For example, the opening passage begins:

> She desired many times that her head might be smitten off with an axe upon a block for the love of our Lord Jesu. Then said our Lord Jesu in her mind: 'I thank thee, daughter, that thou wouldest die for My love; for as often as thou thinkest so, thou shalt have the same meed in heaven as if thou sufferedst the same death, and yet there shall no man slay thee.'[10]

The passages are selected to form a moving and coherent whole, emphasising Margery's devotion to the passion of Christ, and giving a sense of the intimacy of the dialogue between Christ and her soul. Combined with Pepwell's description of Margery, in the heading he gave to these extracts, as an 'ancresse' (religious recluse), they suggested to modern readers that she was perhaps a second Julian of Norwich, that other anchoress whose work has had such an impact on our own day.

In his introduction to the collection, Gardner himself comments on Margery's 'beautiful thoughts and sayings' and, postulating that she lived in the thirteenth or early fourteenth century, describes her as 'a worthy precursor' of Julian. He then deftly encapsulates the impression given by these extracts: 'From the midst of her celestial contemplations, rises up the simple, poignant cry of human suffering: "Lord, for thy great pain have mercy on my little pain." '[11]

Gardner's work was built on by David Knowles in 1927, in his influential study *The English Mystics*, where he puts Margery and Julian together in the same chapter. Like Gardner, he postulates that Margery lived earlier in the fourteenth century than Julian, and so deals with her first. Having reiterated that several passages remind us of Julian, he makes the important assertion: 'And it is clear from others that she was advanced in contemplative prayer.'[12]

AFTER 1934

As we have seen, nothing in the extracts could have prepared twentieth-century readers for the startlingly negative impression created by Margery's complete work, once it had been found. Its contents were made available to the general public by Colonel Butler-Bowdon himself, in a slightly modernised version produced in 1936,[13] and an edition of the original Middle English text was produced in 1940 by Hope Emily Allen and Sandford Brown Meech.[14]

To their astonishment, readers now found that Margery, far from being an anchoress, was a fifteenth-century wife and mother, who had borne fourteen children, before embarking on repeated pilgrimages, both in England and abroad. Her book opens with her suffering a bout of complete insanity. Thereafter, her spirituality took the form of screaming in church, causing disruption all around her. Further, she was several times tried for heresy; on one such occasion, she was also accused of being a secret agent. Less spectacularly, but perhaps more disturbingly in the long run, she seems to have possessed an insensitive, completely self-absorbed, bombastic and rather quarrelsome personality. Finally, her visions and lengthy conversations with Christ, when read in their complete form, turned out to be curiously flat and unconvincing.

Not surprisingly, therefore, her record of her experiences struck many readers as qualitatively different from the writings of the other four medieval mystics. David Knowles, for example, in a later book on the English mystical tradition, reversed his original position and stated roundly that her work 'has little in it of deep spiritual wisdom, and nothing of true mystical experience'.[15] To many, Margery's experiences now seemed to spring from her insanity, and her unattractive personality obscured anything of value in her actual message.

However, these same negative characteristics, which made her so suspect as a mystic half a century ago, are now precisely the elements which make her fascinating to contemporary readers. A wife and mother naturally has a wider appeal in modern society than does a more conventional religious figure without such experience, while a widely travelled person strikes us as adventurous rather than as alarmingly restless or rebellious.

Although she eventually took a vow of celibacy, she did not withdraw at that point into a convent or hermitage, or even, like the great mystic St Catherine of Siena a generation earlier, become a 'tertiary', a member of a religious order while remaining in the world. Instead, she remained more nearly an ordinary person in society than any of the other four 'English mystics', all of whom were either hermits or the counsellors of hermits.

Even her bout of insanity, which continues to provoke the most unease among her readers, has its place in the modern study of the history of mental health.[16] Finally, her loud and disruptive spirituality has been seen as a feminine challenge to male religious assumptions about rigid suppression of the emotions, regimentation, and meek acceptance of male authority.[17]

Margery thus acutely raises the question: What is a mystic? And does the definition of a mystic change over time, so that what was suspect in one age can be seen as valid in another? At any rate, how was Margery judged by the standards of the Middle Ages, and does this tell us anything of interest to us today? Is she simply an example of medieval freakishness?

To evaluate Margery's claim to inclusion in the group of 'English Mystics', this book will first consider in detail the case against her. The charges usually levelled at Margery can be grouped under three main headings, offering three different interpretations of her situation:

1. Her mystical experiences are probably the result of madness, or at least hysteria. She herself relates how she went completely insane for a period after the birth of her first child; her spirituality takes the form of weeping and screaming in public; she manifests throughout the book a difficult and perhaps unbalanced personality; and some of the people who encounter her virulently oppose her and question her genuineness.

2. She is not mad, but she *is* self-deluded, if not an outright

hypocrite, angling for a status for herself in medieval society that she has not been able to achieve through marriage, or through running, as she attempts to do, two businesses of her own. Further, by posing as a mystic, she not only secures this status but engineers for herself an exciting life, marked by high drama: as well as going on repeated journeys abroad, she is three times arrested and tried for heresy.

3. She may be neither mad nor a hypocrite, but a genuinely devout woman, who nonetheless cannot be classed as a mystic: her 'visions' are unconvincing, being largely concerned with herself; her lengthy conversations with Christ are flat and uninspiring; and though she may have derived comfort for herself from the spiritual journey she relates, she has nothing of value to pass on to others.

In examining these charges, we will try to gather up whatever of value in her life and teaching emerges from this process, and then try to pinpoint in what ways she might, in fact, have some distinctive things to say about the relationship between human beings and God.

One

The Nature of the Evidence

BEFORE EMBARKING on a discussion of Margery Kempe's spirituality, we must first marshall all the evidence we have to work on.

External evidence

What we know about Margery Kempe comes almost entirely from her own book, which takes the form of a narrative of her spiritual development over a period of about forty years. Since it necessarily includes a number of external events in her life, some of them quite exciting, it has also been described as the first autobiography in English.[1] Although she herself never mentions the year of any happening, approximate dates have been deduced for her life from the events and public figures she refers to, which can be dated from other sources.

Thus, we deduce that she was born around 1373, and died sometime after 1438, when her book comes to an end, and when she was, she tells us, about sixty years old. A reference to a Margery Kempe in the records of the Guild of the Trinity in King's Lynn, her home town, confirms that she was still alive in 1438.[2] She tells us that she married when she was a little over twenty years old, and bore her first child soon after, presumably around 1394. When she

was about forty, she persuaded her husband to let her live
a life of celibacy; on circumstancial evidence, this has been
dated to 1413.[3] As we shall see further on, her trials for
heresy seem to have taken place in 1417, in connection with
events that can be fairly amply documented elsewhere. In
general, however, she is oblivious to wider political events:
the usurpation of the throne by Henry IV or the Battle of
Agincourt, for example, are not mentioned by her. In this,
Margery is probably typical of the general bulk of the popu-
lation in her time. Apart from the events given above,
therefore, we have no clearly datable fixed points in her
life.

The fact that, on taking her vow of celibacy, she remained
at home with her husband also deprives us of external
records concerning her. Had she become a nun or an
anchoress, we might have the date when she took her vows,
and possibly the date of her death, preserved in the documents of her order. Although the registers of the relevant
bishops have been searched for references to their encounters with her, no evidence has been found; but this is not
surprising, as only certain kinds of business are recorded in
the registers.[4]

As it is, Margery is a valuable example for us of the great
mass of the middle and lower classes of the time, whose
lives left few marks on the official documents of their day.

INTERNAL EVIDENCE: THE PROCESS OF 'WRITING' THE BOOK

When we open Margery's book itself, the first thing we
discover is that it was in fact written for her by a priest, who
had become one of her friends and admirers. It becomes
clear as the narrative progresses that Margery was more or
less illiterate: her parish priest reads works of spirituality to

her, over a period of years (ch. 58); her knowledge of Scripture comes from sermons and from talking to clerics (ch. 14); when she wants to write a letter, she has to get a scribe to do it for her (ch. 18). There is one tantalising glimpse of her holding a book in her hands as she kneels in church (ch. 9), but this probably represents a rudimentary ability to 'follow' devotions which she perhaps knew by heart anyway.

Before studying the words of her book, therefore, we need to consider what this priest-scribe might have contributed to its form and content. Whose presentation of events do we have here, and whose voice are we listening to?

In the 'Proem' at the beginning of the book, Margery's scribe explains how it came to be written. The work is divided into two sections, 'Book I' and 'Book II'. The first section, according to the Proem, was originally the work of an Englishman who had married and settled in Germany, who later lived for a time in Margery's house, and then died. An important article, by John Hirsch,[5] makes a good case for this first scribe being Margery's son. He too had settled in Germany and married there. Late in Margery's narrative, he returns home for an extended visit, accompanied by his wife, but unfortunately dies after only a month. His probable lack of clerical training, combined with illness, would account for the strange condition of this first draft, as described by the priest: it was so badly written, he says, that neither he nor anyone else could decipher much of it, for its language was a peculiar mixture of English and German, and the letters were not shaped and written as letters usually are. Since 'Book I' in fact covers about ninety per cent of the whole work, one might object that a mere month seems an extremely short time for such a labour. However, Margery's account of how little time she had for her usual prayers during the writing of the book (ch. 88) implies that every possible moment was given over to it, conveying a sense of urgency: did she and her son guess that time was short? 'Book II', the work of her main scribe, opens with a description of Margery's son, which further suggests that she might here have been remembering her first scribe.

The second scribe next deciphered and copied out this first draft. At first he was reluctant to make the effort, particularly as Margery had a number of enemies at the time, and he did not wish to get involved. But, he says, divine intervention changed his attitude to Margery and enabled him to make out what was written in the book. As Hirsch points out, there is no trace of the original German-English in what we now have, so the scribe seems in fact to have rewritten, rather than merely copied out, the contents of 'Book I'. He then added, at Margery's dictation, 'Book II', which covers a period of approximately four years between the death of her son and the rewriting of the book.

Are we, then, to ascribe the present content of 'Book I' to the shaping and editing efforts of the priest, with his clerical training? The lack of conventional order in the work would suggest not.

Although the beginning of the work is given some shape by being a narrative of events, even this is not strictly chronological: the story skips about, tracing one strand of spiritual development over several years, before backtracking to pick up a different strand. Thus, we hear about Margery's visit to Julian of Norwich, at a time when she is still bearing children, in chapter 17, some time *after* the moving scene in which her husband agrees to her desire for complete celibacy, in chapter 11. Again, her scribe is reduced to putting a frustrated 'Read chapter 21 first' (when Margery is again pregnant) at the end of chapter 16 (when the Archbishop of Canterbury confirms her vow of celibacy). Later in the *Book*, he says, concerning the cessation of her screaming: 'Although this matter has been written of before this [the great fire in Lynn], nevertheless it happened after this' (ch. 67). This implies that although the scribe might have been motivated by expectations of a smooth sequential narrative, he in fact has had to bow to Margery's way of telling the story, which is based on a different principle: that of association.

Even in the early section of the book, it is clear that Margery is grouping her experiences by subject-matter rather than in chronological sequence. Thus she describes her visit to Julian in the context of her interviews with several other spiritual directors, regardless of whether they came before or after the vow of celibacy. That in turn occurs in a different context, that of a whole package of developments which spring from a crucial spiritual breakthrough, after several years of intense struggle. In the later parts of the book, the sense of chronology gets even hazier, and the grouping by subject-matter more pronounced: similar episodes cluster together, such as examples of her prophetic gifts, her special ministry to the dying, or visions of the passion, although individually they took place in different years.

Consequently, the overall shaping of the work could very well be Margery's, with the underlying principle being, as suggested above, the one of association: one incident reminds her of another, and so on. This would be in keeping with what we might expect of a person used to communicating largely through lengthy conversations (which Margery frequently terms 'dalliance', as in chs 16 and 18), rather than through the necessity of ordering her thoughts on paper, for a less immediate audience. Furthermore, the discernible conflict that she had in this area with her priest-scribe shows that she was capable of coming out on top in a struggle with him, and this is important when we turn to the more detailed question of phrasing and language.

In general, the book's style shows a homely vigour, with many metaphors drawn from domestic life, in a way that is entirely appropriate to a middle-class housewife. In her meditations, for example, she shows a preoccupation with providing Mary and the Christ-child with clean linen; Christ tells her that she will be harassed by others 'as a rat gnaws the stockfish'; a man tells her he would rather be cut up 'as small as meat for the pot' than sleep with her. Now and then, however, the tone changes – usually when some sort of chronological link passage is needed:

> So by process of time her mind and her thought was so joined to God that she never forgot him but continually had him in mind and beheld him in all creatures. And constantly the more she increased in love and devotion, the more she increased in sorrow and contrition, in lowness, in meekness and in the holy dread of our Lord ... (ch. 72).

This kind of rather general, impersonal language could come from any saint's life or sermon of the period, and is typically clerical, or churchy, in tone. It could easily be a didactic insertion by the priest to bring out the significance of the incidents that Margery relates so barely: although full of brief and vivid detail, her narrative is usually strikingly devoid of this sort of comment.

Hirsch also points out that some of the imagery Margery uses in her meditations, particularly in the vision of Christ on the cross which she experiences in Jerusalem (ch. 28), has literary antecedents in the works of St Bernard, Richard Rolle and others. This would suggest reworking by the scribe. However, this kind of imagery was popularised in vernacular works precisely for the benefit of the laity, and includes the highly visual details that someone like Margery is likely to remember. For example, Margery compares the gaping wounds in Christ's body to the many holes in a dovecote, an image indeed found in the writings of St Bernard and Rolle, as Hirsch points out; but it is particularly to be found in Richard Rolle's Meditations on the Passion, written in English,[6] which may well have been widely used among the English laity. It is not necessary to postulate interference by the scribe here.

Apart from the link passages, however, there is another area where a churchy and clerical tone is frequently detected, and that is in the long colloquies, or conversations, between Margery and Christ. These, in contrast to the visions, have rather few striking details or turns of phrase; or, where the phrases are memorable, they are so embedded in the surrounding undistinguished verbiage that we fail to notice them. The colloquies were a major cause of disappointment to readers when Margery's *Book* was first recovered in 1934: as mentioned in the Introduction, they were felt to be uninspiring and overlong, causing William Butler-Bowdon, in the first modernisation of the *Book*, to banish most of them to an Appendix.[7] In these passages, was there perhaps felt a need for decorum which might lead Margery to invite, or at least tolerate, some help in shaping the language from her priest-scribe? This is an issue we shall return to when we discuss the colloquies in more detail.

In general, however, input from the scribe has not had the effect on the manuscript that we might expect: as we have seen, there is no ordering of the material along clear lines, and the whole narrative comes to an extremely abrupt end. By and large, the language has the colour and vigour that we might expect from someone of Margery's powerful though uneducated middle-class background.

There is one further complication: what we have is not the original manuscript, but a copy, made around 1440 (i.e. soon after the completion of the *Book*) by a scribe who has left us his name – Salthows. This suggests someone whose family came from the village of Salthouse in Norfolk, not far from Margery's home town of King's Lynn.[8] It is possible that the copy has smoothed out minute pointers to whether Margery or her original scribe is speaking at any one point. However, we know nothing about Salthows, and there is no reason to assume that he was anything other than a faithful copier of what he had in front of him.

For the present, therefore, while we must grant that the *Book* as we have it is the result of collaboration between Margery and her scribe or scribes, it seems reasonable to proceed on the assumption that hers is the controlling and dominant voice in the *Book*.

TWO

MARGERY'S LIFE: UNRAVELLING ITS CHRONOLOGY

SINCE, AS we have seen, the chronological development of Margery's life is not clear from her own narrative, we will now attempt to establish its broad outlines. This is necessary if we are later to examine the relative importance of the different elements in her life.

THE STEPS OF HER SPIRITUAL CONVERSION

The book opens with the difficult birth of her first child, which takes place when Margery is about twenty-one. She tells us that she conceived soon after she was married at the age of twenty or a little more. After her labour, she is convinced she is about to die, and sends for her confessor, but cannot bring herself to reveal a particular sin on her conscience. Fearing damnation, Margery is driven into a state of insanity, which we would probably now call postpartum psychosis. This state lasts for eight months: 'half year, viii weeks and odd days', a statement which shows that Margery can be specific about duration of time, although she tends to be vague about dates. At last, she is miraculously healed by a beautiful vision of Christ, who, clad in a purple robe, comes to sit on her bed, and asks her one question: 'Daughter, why have you forsaken me, and I never forsook you?' He then slowly ascends into the air, which opens to receive him, and she is immediately restored to full sanity.

This experience, however, does not lead at this point to a spiritual conversion. Coming from a powerful merchant family (her father was both Mayor and Member of Parliament for Lynn, her home town), the young Margery appears to have been chiefly concerned with wealth and status, particularly as shown by her clothes. Being obviously a woman of energy and ambition, she proceeds to set up two businesses in succession, a brewery and a mill. For three or four years her brewery was one of the largest in Lynn, which at this time was a large and prosperous port with important links to the continent. However, things mysteriously go wrong with both businesses.

Perplexed and demoralised by this development, she is now visited by a second intense spiritual experience: one night, in bed, she hears heavenly music. Jumping up, she exclaims, 'Alas that ever I sinned! It is full merry in heaven.' Thereafter, any music or celebration brings on uncontrollable sobbing (chs 1–3).

After this second experience, which seems to occur about fifteen years after the first (hence, around 1408 or 1409),[1] Margery begins an intense life of prayer, going frequently to confession and spending several hours a day in church. She also fasts, wears a hair-shirt, and gives up her concern with outer appearances. Her friends, accusing her of hypocrisy, mostly abandon her. During this period, which seems to last four or five years,[2] Margery also feels an increasing desire to live a life of complete celibacy. However, as a married woman, this is difficult for her: it means gaining her husband's agreement, and as this necessarily commits him, as well as her, to lifelong celibacy within the marriage, it is three years before she can gain his consent. In the meantime, she bears two more children.

In these same years, after an initial two-year period of profound spiritual tranquillity, she is tormented by temptations; ironically, above all by sexual temptations. She describes in convincing detail an episode in which an old friend makes advances to her, and, after a night of torment, during which she ponders on the fact that she cannot bear to be touched by her husband and yet is overwhelmed by sexual desire for this other man, she goes to him to consent. At this point he repulses her, having merely wanted to test her virtue. After this episode, Margery is understandably overcome with humiliation, self-loathing and despair, which lasts, she says, about a year (ch. 4).

Mercifully, a breakthrough occurs 'on a Friday before Christmas Day', when Christ, she states, 'ravished' her soul. In a long colloquy, which is the first of many, he gives a new direction to her life. Having assured her that all her sins are forgiven 'to the utterest point', and that at death she will not go either to hell or to purgatory, he outlines her particular spiritual path: he grants her the gift of lifelong contrition, telling her that he will give her 'a haircloth in her heart'; she is to stop eating meat and to receive Communion every Sunday; she herself will be 'eaten and gnawed' by the world 'as a rat gnaws the stockfish', although she will eventually triumph over all her enemies; and she is to stop saying many prayers and think, rather, such thoughts as Christ will put into her mind. Finally, she is sent to a Dominican anchorite in Lynn for support and direction (ch. 5).

Margery's spiritual life is henceforth marked by similar lengthy colloquies, and by meditations which she appears to report to us as visions. The first of these, for example, opens with Margery asking God what she is to think about, and, in response:

At once she saw St Anne, great with child, and then she begged

St Anne to let her be her maid and her servant. And in due course Our Lady was born, and she [Margery] busied herself to take charge of the child and look after her, until she was twelve years of age, with good food and drink, with fair white clothing and white kerchiefs.

This same meditation goes on to cover the visitation to Elizabeth, the birth of Christ, the adoration of the kings, and the flight into Egypt. Margery is personally involved in some of these scenes, through actions such as buying lodging and bedding for Mary and the child Jesus, and she is warmly commended for her help by Elizabeth (chs 6–8). It is this kind of 'vision' that has contributed to Margery's dubious reputation as a mystic, since her preoccupations are so largely domestic and practical, and there is such a strong emphasis on her own role in the scenes she has set before us.[3] However, there are other ways of viewing these characteristics, as we shall see when we examine the visions in a later chapter.

To this period, when she is just beginning to meditate, also belongs a sequence of vivid and intense dreams, chiefly concerning Mary and the Christ-child (ch. 85), which she does not relate until near the end of the *Book*, but which came, she asserts, at this early point. These intense dreams suggest that the 'breakthrough' was accompanied by a dramatic awakening of her visual imagination, a point we shall return to when discussing her visions in more detail.

A third strand in her spiritual life which is initiated at this point is a prophetic gift, which Margery refers to as her 'revelations', foretelling the salvation or damnation of individuals. However, this particular gift is one Margery would have preferred to be without, as it constrains her to give warning to those heading, as she believes, for damnation, and she constantly doubts her own judgement and fitness for the task. This prophetic gift causes Margery intense suffering; throughout her life it causes her anxiety and self-doubt to the point of near-despair, a state which she seems to associate with her post-partum insanity (chs 23–25; cf. chs 59, 71, 89).

Apart from these spiritual developments, however, Margery also gained a lot of positive outside help and support after the 'breakthrough'. The instruction to go to the Dominican anchorite in Lynn leads her into a whole network of spiritual friendships. In addition to the anchorite himself, she also gets to know the vicar of St Stephen's church in Norwich, whom she goes to see regularly for confession and communion. In Norwich she also visits the Carmelite friar William Southfield, and the noted anchoress Julian (chs 10, 12–13, 17–18). Julian, despite the radically different tone of her own spiritual writings, seems to have recognised Margery as genuine, and gave her sympathetic advice.

Further from home, Margery also goes to other unspecified holy sites, because, Christ tells her, 'My servants desire greatly to see you' (ch. 10). These servants of God, we discover later, include an anchoress in York and a priest, 'Sleytham', at Bridlington (chs 50, 53). Modern scholarship has established that this priest, William Sleightholme, had been the confessor of St John of Bridlington, an Augustinian friar noted for the gift of spiritual weeping;[4] we thus get a glimpse of an informal association, criss-crossing England, of priests, hermits and lay-people sharing common forms of spiritual experience. The support of this network is an enduring characteristic of Margery's life, and has to be set against the bitter opposition that she also encountered.

After the 'breakthrough', Margery's desire for celibacy also seems to have been granted within a few months. In a moving scene when Margery and her husband are returning from York one midsummer eve (23 June, probably in 1413),[5] they reach agreement on this matter (ch. 11). That it was real agreement, not just a grudging assent on John Kempe's part, is shown by the generosity with which he thereafter accompanies her on many of her journeys in England, protecting her reputation by his presence and supporting her when she has to defend her way of life before powerful clerics. In particular, they go together first to the Bishop of Lincoln, and then to the Archbishop of Canterbury, for ecclesiastical ratification of their vow.

Margery needs this support from her husband, given that by now she has embarked on a somewhat unusual and conspicuous style of existence: as we have seen, she travels extensively within England in search of expert counsel and direction, she stands out for her refusal to eat meat, and she wishes to wear white as a sign of her celibacy. The sort of danger she runs is exemplified at Canterbury, where she is not only reviled by the monks, but nearly lynched by the mob as a Lollard (ch. 13).[6]

JOURNEYS ABROAD

Soon after gaining her husband's consent to her vow of celibacy, Margery sets out on a long journey abroad, lasting in all about eighteen months (1413–15). She goes on pilgrimage to the Holy Land, crossing first to Holland, then travelling overland down through Switzerland to Venice, and from there crossing to Palestine by ship. Other English pilgrims who set out with her from Yarmouth are vituperative and extraordinarily cruel to her, and continue to be so whenever she meets up with them later (chs 26–43).

It is during her visit to the Holy Sepulchre at Jerusalem, when she intensely relives the scenes of the Lord's passion and mentally beholds him hanging on the cross, that she

adds to her already disruptive spiritual weeping the further
phenomenon of crying out, that is, shouting, writhing and
even screaming (ch. 28).

She returns via Assisi and Rome, where she makes a stay
of about six months. These months are a particularly fertile
period in Margery's spiritual life. During this time she
experiences a mystical marriage to the Godhead (ch. 35),
and now feels free to wear the white clothes she had been
wanting to adopt for some time. This spiritual marriage has
important consequences: from this point on, Margery will
be dogged by poverty and ill-health; she will experience
various mystical phenomena of a physical sort; and, most
significantly, she will develop her own mystical view of the
world and of the human life around her. A vision of St
Jerome also confirms her special vocation to weeping, which
she sees as a ministry for others.

While in Italy, she makes new spiritual friends, such as
Richard the humpback, a beggar who accompanies her from
Assisi, and a German priest in Rome who knows no English,
but is miraculously enabled to understand her and can thus
act as her confessor (chs 33, 40). He orders her to look
after a poor widow in Rome, which she does for six weeks.
Moving about among the poor of the city, she feels impelled
to give away all her money, in order to experience the
destitution and nakedness of Christ.

Fortunately, charitable people such as the rich lady
Margaret Florentine, whom she had also met on the road
from Assisi, make sure she has food. And the Italian women
in general treat her with compassion and kindness, though
it is not clear from Margery's account whether this is because
they consider her a holy woman or simply deranged by some
affliction.

Back in England after this long journey abroad, Margery's
experience of destitution continues: she is poor and in debt,

and it is a cold winter. She has such a severe bout of illness that she is thought to be dying and is anointed. Meanwhile, her recently adopted white clothes, combined with the shouting in church that she had first experienced in Jerusalem, provoke hostility to her among the townspeople of Lynn.

After about two years, she determines to go to Compostela in Spain, and various people give her enough money to enable her to do so. However, this is a much shorter trip; although she has to wait six weeks in Bristol for a ship, she is actually away for about four weeks. This journey probably takes place in the summer of 1417 (chs 43–5).

Although these foreign travels are very important in Margery's spiritual development, and the scene of some intense inner experiences, she tells us so little externally about the places she visits that these journeys are a slightly disappointing part of her work. Whereas other parts of the *Book* give us an almost cinematic sense of the medieval world in which she lived, with a string of vivid vignettes, the scenes set abroad are curiously flat and monochrome. For instance, there is only one of her usually lively details in her account of the Holy Land: when, as usual, her fellow pilgrims refused to help her struggle up the mount of Christ's temptation in the wilderness, a handsome Saracen supported her all the way to the top. On her way to the Holy Land, it is her relations with the other pilgrims which preoccupy her, not the foreign countries through which she passes; further, these fellow pilgrims are curiously one-dimensional, animated by a sustained malice towards her which lacks adequate explanation. In Italy, as we have seen, a number of people are very close to her, but there is not one visual detail about Italy, Rome or Assisi themselves. She does, however, specify the churches in Rome where some of her important experiences took place, such as St John Lateran and St Maria Maggiore. About Compostela in Spain she tells us nothing at all.

However, Margery herself stresses, in connection with a later journey, that she concentrated more on contemplation than on details such as place-names (Book II, ch. 4). In other words, her focus is internal, not external, and she is not writing a guide-book. Further, it is clear that it is other individuals who matter to her, not relatively impersonal phenomena such as buildings and places. Her critics, on the other hand, see here a worrying lack of response to external reality, a lack of normal curiosity about new experiences and environments, which confirms them in their view of Margery as unhealthily self-absorbed and unbalanced.

TRIALS FOR HERESY

On her second return to England, after her brief sojourn in Compostela, Margery is almost immediately arrested several times in quick succession, and interrogated as a heretic in various ecclesiastical courts, chiefly in Leicester and York. These trial scenes, unlike the foreign journeys, are detailed and vivid, and form some of the most satisfyingly constructed and dramatic incidents in the book. For instance, to the Archbishop of York's accusation, 'I hear you are a right wicked woman', she retorts, 'And I hear you are a right wicked man.'

Taking the arrests in order, we find her landing at Bristol, and then travelling to the shrine of Hailes in Gloucestershire, where there was a relic of the blood of Christ. She then decides to go to York, but on the way, in Leicester, she is arrested by the Mayor and taken before the Earl's Steward. After an imprisonment of three weeks, she is then examined fully by the Abbot and Dean of Leicester, who clear her of heresy and release her.

Nothing daunted, she continues to York, where she spends two weeks relatively unmolested, before being summoned before the Cathedral Chapter. She is sent on to the Archbishop of York at Cawood. After a prolonged and difficult examination she is again cleared, and continues her interrupted stay in York.

She then heads south, on her way home, but is rearrested at Hull by servants of the Duke of Bedford, and taken to Beverley. By chance, the Archbishop of York also arrives in Beverley, and is clearly exasperated to find her being brought before him again. Released a third time, she is rearrested on the other side of the Humber, but this time is allowed to continue on her way without further interrogation.

A final incident occurs, a few weeks or possibly a few months later, when she and her husband, having gone to London to obtain a certificate of her orthodoxy from the Archbishop of Canterbury, are arrested near Ely on their way back; fortunately, the Archbishop's certificate has the desired effect.

All these arrests occur within a period of weeks, most of them in September 1417. Obviously, there is some particular agitation about heretics at this moment, and this will be explored further in the chapter devoted to these trials.

KING'S LYNN

We now come to by far the longest period in Margery's spiritual odyssey, the fifteen years between 1418 and 1433, when she appears to settle down more or less quietly in Lynn. This is the period in which Margery and her scribe have abandoned any attempt at chronology, and yet references to events occurring before or after other events show that this period, too, had its phases. An attempt to disentangle them produces the following outline.

On Margery's return to Lynn, she enters on a period of recurrent illness. As also occurred on her return from Rome, she is so ill that she receives the last rites. Though she recovers, she is afflicted for eight years with pains in her side, head and back, so intense that, she significantly tells us, she feared to lose her wits; when these pains cease, her spiritual shouting and roaring intensifies.

These manifestations earn her increasing hostility, particularly from a noted Franciscan preacher, whom a marginal note in the manuscript identifies as Richard Melton. Until then, the Dominicans had helpfully solved the problem of her disruptive screaming in church, by giving her communion in their own chapel, but when the Dominican anchorite who had been her chief adviser dies, they withdraw their support. This exacerbates the situation, as Margery now has to be given communion in the parish church; here her cries are so loud that they can be heard even in the street outside. One of her closest friends, the Carmelite friar Master Aleyn, is forbidden to speak to her by the Provincial of his order. At some point too, the vicar of St Stephen's in Norwich, one of her first supporters, has also died, so that Margery is left almost without friends.

However, she gains other allies. A new priest comes to Lynn, who reads to her over a period of seven or eight years from the Bible and its commentaries, and from the spiritual classics of the day – the works of Rolle, Hilton, Bonaventure, and Bridget of Sweden – which Margery had already referred to in her first conversation with the vicar of St Stephen's, Norwich (cf. ch. 17).

Margery's scribe interpolates a personal comment here: he too had been turned from her by Richard Melton, but was brought back to her side by these works of Rolle and

Bonaventure, and then by the life of Marie d'Oignies (ch. 62).[7]

Others stand up for her, too: a visiting Dominican, who is a doctor of divinity, bears her interruptions of his own sermons patiently; the Bishop of Norwich shows similar forbearance; and another cleric instructs the people to judge her charitably.

During this time of controversy, Margery strengthens her position by working a minor miracle: when, in 1421, a fire burns down the Guildhall in Lynn and threatens to engulf the parish church, Margery's prayers avert disaster, by apparently bringing down an unseasonal fall of snow to damp the flames. Her cries and shouts also are given a positive value by the people of Lynn when she is asked to pray at the bedside of the dying: here her commission to pray for all sinners, and her general stress on contrition, find an outlet in a highly appropriate form of ministry. At some point she also heals a woman, who, like herself, had gone insane after childbirth.

She is also gaining a considerable reputation as a kind of prophet, owing to her 'revelations', already mentioned, concerning various persons' sins and whether they are destined for heaven or hell. With her acute sense of the reality of damnation, these revelations cause her, as we have seen, great anguish and self-doubt; during one of these periods of doubt she is tormented for twelve days by visions of male genitals, an episode that has been frequently cited as showing that she suffered from sexual repression. Meanwhile, she continues to have vivid 'contemplations', describing in gory detail scenes such as the scourging of Christ, his stripping before being nailed to the cross, and the mourning of his female followers over his dead body.

Eventually, when opposition to her has reached such a pitch that her friends are counselling her to leave Lynn,

Christ takes her loud shouting from her, leaving her with only her original, quieter gift of abundant tears. This immediately produces the almost inevitable charge of hypocrisy: her detractors promptly assume that she has been putting on her cries all along, and that she has at last been cowed by Melton's denunciations of her from the pulpit.

Later in the book, Margery herself links this development with an inner transition from devotion to the manhood of Christ to greater contemplation of his Godhead (ch. 85). Owing to her hazy sense of time passing, it is difficult to work out when this important cessation in her shouting occurred. However, at one point she refers to her cries lasting ten years, which would bring us to around 1425.

The final phase that can be distinguished in this period is the one when she had to nurse her husband through the last years of his life. A disastrous fall leaves him disabled and eventually senile, and she finds his double incontinence hard to bear. Fortunately, at the very end of this phase, she is gladdened by a visit from her grown-up son, who has settled in Germany and married there. He has undergone a religious conversion, and comes home to visit his mother with his wife, though they leave their tiny daughter in Germany. Her son dies of a sudden illness after only a month, and her husband soon after, but Margery's daughter-in-law remains with her a further eighteen months. During this last phase, as we saw in the previous chapter, Margery also embarks upon the dictation of her book.

HER LAST JOURNEY ABROAD

In 'Book II', which amounts to hardly more than an afterword, Margery's third foreign journey takes place when she accompanies her daughter-in-law back to Danzig, around

Easter 1433. Their ship is blown off course and lands briefly
on the Norwegian coast, but they reach Germany without
further mishap. Margery stays about six weeks, and then
returns to England, via centres of pilgrimage at Wilsnack
in Brandenburg, Stralsund in Pomerania, and Aachen. As
before, she meets with both kindness and harshness on
her travels, which this time are made more difficult by the
infirmity of age, for she is by now over sixty. Her return to
England, after an absence of about three months, abruptly
closes the narrative.

There then follows a sort of appendix, comprising a series
of prayers which reflect her practice for many years after
she had been to the Holy Land, but before her loud cries
had ceased.

In summary, then, we can discern the following pattern
in the twenty-five years of Margery's life after her final conversion: five years of intense prayer and asceticism; four
years during which she makes two journeys abroad
(1413–17); a few weeks of trials for heresy (1417); fifteen
years of stable life in King's Lynn; and a third journey abroad
of a few months (1433).

It is important to note the different proportions in her
life of these various activities. As we shall see in the following
chapters, various criticisms are levelled at Margery, some of
which imply that she was regularly tried for heresy
throughout her life, or that she went on frequent journeys
abroad. Our first task, therefore, has been to get these
aspects of her life into proper perspective, by establishing
this chronological outline of her life.

We are left with the question: What happened to Margery
after she returned from Danzig? In the light of her fifteen
years of stability in Lynn, which in fact occupy the major
part of the spiritual life she recounts in her *Book*, and given
that we leave her as a widow, without family obligations,

perhaps we should not dismiss too hastily the description given her by Henry Pepwell in 1521: 'Margerie kempe ancresse of lynn.' After the completion of her book, perhaps she did eventually regularise her situation by withdrawing to an anchorhold, or by being in some way officially committed to the solitary life within her own home.

Three

MADNESS

As we saw in the Introduction, critics who reject Margery's mysticism as genuine usually level charges at her which can be loosely grouped under three main headings. The first of these was that her mystical experiences are the product of outright madness, or at least some pin-pointable condition: for instance, E. Colledge, writing in 1966, postulates that she was 'a hysteric, if not an epileptic'.[1] And indeed, at first glance, there is much to suggest that there is something clinically wrong with Margery's mind or psyche.

We have seen that Margery's mystical life begins with a psychotic episode after the birth of her first child. It is this, combined with her sobbing and screaming in church, that has attracted to her the accusation of outright madness.

THE PSYCHOTIC EPISODE

In examining this accusation, it is important to note that there is only one psychotic episode in Margery's life, and its contents are quite different from those of any of her subsequent 'visions' or conversations with Christ.

In her madness, she saw devils with flaming mouths trying to swallow her, and urging her to give up her Christian faith, abandon all virtues and good deeds, and turn against her family and all her friends. And she says that she gave in to them: she slandered her husband and her friends, and also turned her hatred on herself, uttering not only many vicious words against herself but also trying to commit suicide by self-mutilation. On one occasion, she bit her own hand so violently that she bore the scar for the rest of her life. Eventually, she had to be bound night and day to her bed to stop her killing herself, and even then, she says, she tried to tear open the skin above her heart with her fingernails. This state lasted a little over eight months.

The healing vision of Christ which terminated this period is to be distinguished, most readers would agree, from the psychotic episode itself. It took place at a moment when she was alone, her keepers being momentarily out of the room, and has a notable simplicity and brevity: Christ, dressed in a purple robe, sat on the side of her bed and asked her, 'Daughter, why have you forsaken me, and I never forsook you?'. As we shall see when we look at Margery's later visions, this first one has an air of authenticity that nothing in her later life quite matches. The cure which accompanied it was correspondingly instantaneous and total.

The first point to notice about this time of madness is that it is in no way a foundation for what follows. Her subsequent visions are all of Christ, Mary and the disciples, and not of devils, and she does not hear again any temptations against her faith or against goodness and virtue.

The second point to make is that no one is in any doubt that this madness is entirely a terrible affliction; Margery herself, and all those around her, regard it as evil, and her keepers are sensibly sceptical about the immediacy of her healing. When she asks to be given the keys of the foodstore, in order to help herself to food and drink, they are reluctant, on the grounds that she does not know what she is saying and would probably give everything away. John Kempe, however, has faith in her and overrules t̶ when

Hoccleve → skepticism

she later begins to go on pilgrimage to places within England, it is partly to give thanks 'inasmuch as she was cured'. No one, then, is confusing this psychotic episode with a mystical experience.

Furthermore, this episode is not usually one of the elements that readers find unattractive in Margery. On the contrary, this opening of her narrative usually elicits immediate sympathy and interest. One of the studies which shows most respect for Margery, Roy Porter's, concentrates on this part of her experience.[2] He also points out that she continued to be fearful of a relapse, and this observation is worth looking at in some detail.

FEAR OF RELAPSE

She seems to view her period of insanity primarily as a time of despair, and she tells us that she was tempted to despair at several subsequent periods. The imminence of despair seems to be the key factor, and is probably to be distinguished from her state of mind when 'she feared to have lost her wits', during a period of intense pain and illness after her return to England from Compostela (ch. 56). In that episode, Margery does not elaborate on her fear, but rather goes on to show how she prayed intimately to God during the periods of pain which afflicted her head and back, and how she vividly visualised the Lord's passion. It is from this passage that comes the phrase 'Lord, for your great pain have mercy on my little pain', which so struck Edmund Gardner. But when despair raises its head, Margery connects it with attacks from the devil and/or punishment from God. This applies chiefly to the times when she was deeply troubled by her prophetic gift.

When first describing these prophetic insights, or 'feelings' as she terms them (chs 23–5), Margery runs through a catalogue of briefly told incidents in which it was revealed to her whether someone seriously ill would live or die. On one occasion she was even informed that a newly deceased person was in purgatory. This catalogue ends with the following comment:

> These feelings, and many others more than are written here, concerning both living and dying, of some to be saved and some to be damned, were to this creature great pain and punishment. She would have preferred to have suffered any bodily penance than these feelings, if she could have put them aside, because of the dread that she had of deceits and illusions from her spiritual foes. She had at times such great trouble with these feelings when they did not accord with her understanding, that her confessor feared that she might have fallen into despair on account of them. And then, after her trouble and her great fear, it would be shown to her soul in what manner her feelings should be understood. (ch. 23)

We see here Margery's ongoing fear of 'deceits and illusions' from the devil, mankind's spiritual enemy, and the temptation to despair. This ongoing fear of deceit is an important element in Margery's spiritual journey, as we shall see when we look at her constant seeking of reassurance from every person of spiritual authority who crosses her path.

In the matter of the acute doubt that she felt when her prophetic intuition did not seem to fit in with her general understanding, the pre-eminent incident is the one when she was tormented for twelve days by visions of male genitals (ch. 59). She sees this as a punishment for not having trusted what her prophetic gift was telling her. On this occasion she had decided that intimations that certain people were damned could not come from God, but rather from 'some evil spirit' determined to 'deceive' her. Because of this resistance and unbelief, she says, the Lord withdrew all holy thoughts from her and permitted her to have evil thoughts. She goes on:

> And so the Devil made play with her, dallying with her with accursed thoughts, just as our Lord dallied with her before with holy thoughts. And just as she had before had many glorious visions and high contemplation . . . right so she now had horrible and abominable sights, in spite of anything she could do, of men's organs and other abominations.

She sees many priests and members of religious orders coming before her and exposing themselves to her, while the devil urges her to choose whom she will sleep with first, as she must have sex with all of them. And she acknowledges that these suggestions were 'delectable to her against her will', although she does strenuously resist assenting to them. Although she confesses these thoughts and receives absolution, 'she found no release until she was nearly at the point of despair'.

At this point she prays to know why God has gone back on his promise not to forsake her – an important clue that she associates this experience with her earlier time of madness, which, as we saw above, ended with Christ's words to her, 'I never forsook you'. She is told that this is a punishment for not believing that her prophetic gifts come from God, and that she must bear these sexual visions, which torment her even when she is attending the sacrament, for a full twelve days. After that time, they leave her as suddenly and completely as they had come. Margery comments that during this time she thought she was in hell.

This incident has been made much use of in modern attempts to explain Margery's spirituality in terms of some kind of sexual problem, as we shall see. What is notable here, however, is that Margery understands this experience in terms of a specific punishment for a specific failure, rather than as an ongoing temptation arising from her own fleshly lusts. The fixed duration of the experience, which lasts no more and no less than the pre-ordained twelve days, underlines this character of chastisement from God. Moreover, Margery is not the only medieval mystic to have had this particular kind of tormenting vision. Catherine of Siena had a similar experience early in her spiritual life.[3]

In general, one might argue that these experiences of near-despair combine with Margery's profound awe of God to exert a kind of relentless pressure on her mind, which is accepted by Margery as an ongoing purging of her sins. Christ says to her:

> I have chastised you myself as I wished by many great dreads and torments that you have had with evil spirits, both sleeping and waking, for many years . . . It is a great grace and miracle that you have your bodily senses, given the vexation that you have had with them before now. I have also, daughter, chastised you with the fear of my Godhead, and many times have I filled you with fear through great tempests of winds, so that you thought vengeance would have fallen on you for sin. (ch. 22)

In this whole matter of near-insanity, then, Margery demonstrates a crystalline honesty and simplicity. She is quite clear that her madness is to be distinguished from her 'holy thoughts', and her cleaving to God is partly fuelled by the fear that she might relapse into her initial psychotic state.

However, if anything, her experience gives her a positive role in the eyes of many readers: she can be seen as a sympathetic example of someone who lived out her life in the aftermath of mental illness, possibly under a certain ongoing fear of relapse, but who nonetheless was able to function competently in everyday life, while also engaging in an intense spiritual life.

PROBLEMS OF PERSONALITY

It is the rest of Margery's behaviour that is the problem: her
screaming in church, her visions, and her sometimes difficult relationships with other people. On the other hand,
the early-fourteenth-century mystic Richard Rolle also
screamed, experienced mystical bodily phenomena, and had
head-on collisions with his detractors,[4] but no one has
sought to label him hysterical or epileptic, as they have with
Margery. On the contrary, both in his own day and down
the centuries, he has often been reputed the greatest of the
English mystics. It seems, rather, that some less obvious
factor virtually drives readers to seek some medical explanation for her experiences, and this factor may have
something to do with a powerful strand of unawareness and
self-advertisement in Margery's make-up.

These two traits manifest themselves in her whole way of
relating to others. Although she recovers her sanity, for the
rest of her life she appears to go out of her way to attract
attention: as we have seen, she eventually adopts white
clothing as a public sign of her vow of chastity, and her
shouting in church disrupts the services.

Further, she tends to view all her human contacts in terms
of best friends and worst enemies, rating their holiness
according to their attitude to her. It does not seem to occur
to Margery that some of the opposition she encounters
might not be to Christ within her, but to her own unreason-
able behaviour. In one incident, Margery gets into what can
only be described as a schoolgirl fight with a widow in Lynn.
This woman had rejected Margery's advice that she should
abandon her own confessor in favour of Margery's, and in
the ensuing quarrel had forbidden Margery the house. The
text continues:

Then our Lord bade this creature [Margery] to have a letter

> written and to send it to her. A master of divinity wrote a
> letter at the request of this creature and sent it to the widow with
> these clauses that follow. One clause was that the widow would
> never have the grace that this creature had. Another was that
> if this creature never came to her house again it would please
> God right well. (ch. 18)

The letter seems to have no practical purpose, and Margery
seems completely unaware of anything questionable in her
motivation for writing it. Margery's statement that it was
Christ who commanded her to send this letter might cause
one to question the genuineness of this divine injunction;
and if this injunction is dubious, what of others?

According to Margery, Christ forcefully tells her several
times that a person's response to her is identical with their
response to him: 'Those who honour you, honour me; those
who despise you, despise me, and I shall chastise them for
it. I am in you and you in me. And those who hear you,
hear the voice of God.' (ch. 10). Or, about an English priest
who opposed her in Rome: 'Though he ran every year to
Jerusalem I have no liking for him, for as long as he speaks
against you, he speaks against me.' (ch. 34). Or again, she
reports about Richard Melton: 'My Lord tells me that he is
angry with him, and he says to me that it would be better if
he had never been born, for he despises his works in me.'
(ch. 63).

There is good New Testament precedent for this attitude
of Margery's, in the instructions of Jesus to the apostles: 'He
that receives you, receives me, and he that receives me,
receives the one who sent me' (Matthew 10:40). There is
also a sense, as I hope to show, in which Margery could
indeed have a role as a sign of God. Nonetheless, what
most readers have seen in such statements is an undue
preoccupation with her own spiritual status, conceived of in
rather competitive terms: she is better than the widow to

whom she writes the letter, and God is angry with Melton, despite his holy reputation (ch. 63), because of his attitude to Margery. Indeed, this preoccupation strikes some critics as her dominant one, and her relationship with God as a pose to secure this status. Perhaps, though, it is simply characteristic of Margery that, in her eagerness to obey, she understands and enacts too crudely and offensively the injunctions which she genuinely receives.

Two other aspects of Margery's rather problematic behaviour can be examined through the lens of her visit to Julian of Norwich. Julian speaks to her at length on two topics: the need for her to trust the guidance of the Holy Spirit in her soul, and the need for her to practise patience.

Julian's first point is perhaps a response to what strikes many readers as the most obvious self-advertising aspect of Margery's behaviour: her constant retelling of her experiences, and of her whole life, to any person of spiritual authority who crosses her path, both in England and abroad. Margery's motives for this constant retelling are not always clear: in Constanza, for example, on her way to the Holy Land, she makes a general confession to the Pope's Legate, showing him her life 'from the beginning unto that hour' because, she says, 'he was the Pope's legate and a worshipful clerk' (ch. 27). It seems she needs affirmation from the most powerful person around, and will hunt out that person to get it.

Usually, however, she says she shows various priests her 'feelings' in order to 'see if there was any deceit in them'. As we have seen, her ongoing fear of deceit by the devil seems to have been a serious anxiety to her, and Katherine Cholmeley and Edward Watkin, two of Margery's earliest defenders after the rediscovery of her book, have both seen here the humble self-doubt of a Teresa of Avila. Most readers, however, far from being struck by a likeness to St

Teresa, have seen here an obsessive self-disclosure more akin to bragging than humility.

Consequently, when Julian, echoing the Epistle of James, says to her, 'He that is evermore doubting is like to the flood of the sea, which is moved and born about with the wind, and that man is not likely to receive the gifts of God', perhaps she is trying to contain this neurotic self-doubt and constant self-revelation. Indeed, as far as we can deduce from the text, on this same visit to Norwich Margery has already poured out her soul to the vicar of St Stephen's church and to the Carmelite friar William Southfield.

From Margery's account, Julian seems to have recognised her as authentic, for the two women had several days of conversation together. Perhaps the older woman, whose own writings so emphasise compassion, could discern both Margery's genuine fear of deceit and the ultimately unhelpful nature of her repeated consultations with a great variety of counsellors.

When Julian moves on to her second point, the text, which has reported most of Julian's advice indirectly, in summary, passes into direct speech. This second point therefore emerges with all the more force:

> I pray God grant you perseverance. Set all your trust in God and fear not the speech of the world, for the more scorn, shame and reproof that you have in the world the more is your merit in the sight of God. Patience is necessary to you, for in that shall you preserve your soul.

Patience, in medieval thought, was an aspect of fortitude, and what Julian is here counselling is probably the kind of calm endurance and non-reaction to others' remarks which will help Margery to withstand opposition.

Margery's attempts at patience, however, have an unfortunate effect on those on whom she practises it. The most sustained example of this is in her relationship with her fellow pilgrims on her way to the Holy Land. Things begin to go wrong at Yarmouth, when her 'meek' reply to their angry requests to her to behave normally makes them even angrier. In the face of their continuing hostility, she adopts the role of long-suffering humility, always taking the lowest place at table and saying nothing – so much so that when the Papal Legate comes to dine with the pilgrims at Constanza, he asks her, 'Why are you no merrier?'. To provoke such a question, her silence cannot have come across as simple self-effacement. Rather, it must have spoken volumes.

HYSTERIA AND SEXUALITY

It is this strong element of self-advertisement even in the face of opposition, and her preoccupation with her spiritual status in the eyes of others, that has led modern commentators to postulate for her a basically hysterical personality, in the clinical sense. The classic, decidedly thought-provoking, statement on Margery as having a hysterical personality organisation is probably that of Dr Anthony Ryle, given at some length in Stephen Medcalf's *The Later Middle Ages*[5] and reprinted in Barry Windeatt's notes to his Penguin translation of Margery.[6] Dr Ryle sees in her a persistent preoccupation with some kind of sexual guilt, perhaps linked with the unconfessed sin which brings on her initial bout of insanity. Her subsequent behaviour, in which she poses as a person with a special relationship to God, then becomes a defence against this preoccupation. Dr Ryle feels her claims are probably spurious, because, despite her attempts at visionary writing, her chief concern seems to be with the view that others had of her as a religious person. Any rejection of her claims she could experience as persecution, thus rendering her view of the situation impenetrable to outside criticism.

Persuasively coherent as this interpretation of Margery is, one of its chief problems is that Margery did, in fact, eventually confess the sin that had so plagued her. When she was finally converted, she tells us, 'she was shriven sometimes two or three times a day, and in particular of that sin which she had so long concealed and hidden, as is written in the beginning of the book.' (ch. 3). The complete change of goals and values in her life, and her abundant weeping, might then be seen as signs of release from guilt, rather than as a continuing compensation for it. Confirmation of this release comes at the beginning of chapter 15, when she begins to feel the urge to go to the Holy Land: 'This creature, when our Lord had forgiven her her sin, as is written before, had a desire to see the places where he was born . . .'.

Our problem is that Margery does not at any point tell her readers what that great sin was, so we are left guessing. The tendency has been to assume that it has something to do with sexuality; Dr Ryle, for example, refers to Margery's near-relapse at the time that she is tormented by the visions of male genitals. This view, that Margery's entire spirituality is in some way connected with sexual unease, has been supported by other writers, such as Trudy Drucker, who also diagnoses hysteria, but refers to its more traditional sense of being allied to frustrated child-bearing. In this case, the approved therapy is 'provision of the opportunity for healthy expression of the reproductive instinct', which fails to take into account the fact that Margery has borne fourteen children.[7]

It is difficult to determine, however, to what extent there really were sexual problems in Margery's life. She herself tells us that she had an intensely satisfying sexual relationship with John Kempe: when she first asks him to agree to a life of celibacy, she argues that 'they often-times, she well knew, had displeased God by their inordinate love and the great delectation that each of them had in using the other;' now they should both abstain from the lust of their bodies (ch. 3).

In considering the state of sexual abstinence spiritually preferable to that of physical marriage, Margery is simply typical of her age. Christ himself, in chapter 21, repeats to her the standard medieval teaching that the state of virginity is the most perfect and holy, the state of widowhood ranks second, and marriage comes third.[8] It is interesting, however, that Christ does not entirely endorse her view that her sexual relations with John Kempe are a barrier to her life of prayer. When she says, also in chapter 21, that she is not worthy to hear the Lord speak while still having sex with her husband, even though it is unwelcome to her, Christ assures her that for that reason it is not a sin for her. While commending her desire for chastity, he assures her that he loves married women just as well as virgins, and in particular, 'I love you as well as any virgin in the world.'

As we have seen, John and Margery's passionate love-making resulted in the bearing of fourteen children. At present it has become fashionable to consider that most of these children were born against Margery's will, but when we consider that her conversion, and her corresponding loss of sexual desire, took place about fifteen years after the opening of her book, and that her husband agreed to her request 'three or four years' after she had first made it, it seems more likely that the majority of these children were conceived during the years in which she experienced 'great delectation' in the physical side of her marriage. Of course, this does not alter the fact that the last three or four years of her sexual relationship with John Kempe were extremely painful to her; it is also clear that she did bear at least one child during this time (ch. 21).

Modern readers are also surprised by her silence about her children in the rest of her book; apart from telling us about the visit of her adult son near the end of her narrative, she never mentions any of them, not even to tell us whether they all survived, or of what sex they were. However, it is likely that if many of them had died, Margery would have mentioned this as yet another element going wrong in her life in the period before her conversion, when her two businesses failed; and after her conversion, she might have seen this as yet another trial or chastisement sent by God. Instead, when she has to defend herself before the ecclesiastical authorities, she always refers to her bearing of fourteen children with a kind of sturdy pride (e.g. ch. 48). Let us hope this indicates that, by and large, things went well for her children. In any case, in not mentioning them, Margery is not necessarily untypical of her age.

What of Margery's sexual experience, if any, before marriage? She swears on oath before the Abbot of Leicester that she never in her life had intercourse with any man other than her husband (ch. 48). Her unconfessed sin, therefore, could not actually have been a pre-marital affair. On the other hand, perhaps modern research into the long-term effects of sexual abuse in childhood will eventually throw clearer light on this matter. Whereas earlier critics looked simply for signs of sexual *repression* in Margery, future critics may look rather for more subtle signs of sexual *confusion*: perhaps Margery experienced before marriage some kind of sexual interference, short of full intercourse, which caused her to feel ambivalent about her sexual nature. The constant self-disclosure which we examined above could suggest insecure personal boundaries, which might also be the result of some such invasion of her personality as a child or an adolescent.

However, it is our age which puts enormous emphasis on sex. Stephen Medcalf reminds us that Margery's sin could have belonged to a different realm altogether.[9] He points out that the priest of her local parish, William Sawtre, was the first man to be burned in England under legislation brought in to combat the Lollard heresy, in 1401. Medcalf dates the birth of Margery's first child to around 1400, which is roughly six years later than most commentators would now accept, so the intimate connection that he postulates between the burning of Sawtre and Margery's breakdown probably did not occur. Nonetheless, his is a timely reminder that doctrinal error was perhaps a worse sin in medieval eyes than any sexual irregularity. Other serious matters were bearing false witness and financial dishonesty. It is really only the emphasis on hysteria that has led people to speculate that Margery's sin was sexual.

Apart from postulating a certain sexual unease in Margery, however, the diagnosis of hysteria focuses on what many people would instinctively label 'hysterical' behaviour: her loud weeping and screaming in public places, under the influence of some strong emotion. It is this weeping and screaming that we will turn to in the next chapter.

Four

TEARS AND SCREAMING

Margery's weeping seems to spring from several different emotional sources within her. These can be roughly classified as penitence for her own sins; penitence for the sins of the world; and compassion for the sufferings of Christ.

Almost immediately after her conversion (which takes place when she hears heavenly music, about fifteen years after her recovery from madness) she finds herself sobbing when she carefully reviews the sins of her whole life, from her childhood up (ch. 3). Since she conducts this review 'full many a time', she spends much time weeping, and already she finds herself in trouble with her neighbours: 'Her weeping was so plentiful and so continuous that many people thought that she could weep or stop weeping at will.' Margery tells us that she formed the habit of rising at two or three in the morning and spending many hours in church praying, both until noon and also after noon; consequently, much of this weeping must have been public.

This sobbing for her sins seems to have lasted steadily during the four or so years which precede the spiritual breakthrough, on the Friday before Christmas Day, when her soul is ravished by Christ (ch. 5). Although he assures her that her sins are completely forgiven, and that she will go neither to hell nor to purgatory, this strand of personal contrition does not cease. On the contrary, Christ assures her that she will have the gift of contrition until the end of her life, and that, in place of the hair-shirt she has been wearing and which he now commands her to remove, he will give her a hair-shirt in her heart.

This inner, more hidden contrition then rapidly widens out to encompass sorrow for sin in general. Her weeping is 'sometimes for her own sin, sometimes for the sin of the people' (ch. 7), and Christ tells her: 'I have ordained you to kneel before the Trinity to pray for all the world, for many hundred thousand souls shall be saved by your prayers.' Margery's weeping thus takes on an intercessory character, and this particular theme grows steadily stronger throughout the rest of her *Book*. The offensiveness of all sin to God is for Margery an overwhelming reality, which she feels we should all be deeply aware of. Christ says to her at one point, 'If you saw the sin of the people as I do, you would have much more wonder at my patience and much more sorrow for the sin of the people than you have.' (ch. 20). She asks God for 'a well of tears to constrain you with', so that no man need suffer damnation for his sins. She goes on, with one of her vigorous homely analogies: 'If I could, Lord, give the people contrition and weeping . . . as easily as I could give them a penny from my purse, I would quickly fill men's hearts with contrition so that they might cease from their sin.' (ch. 57).

On a more individual basis, we see Margery developing a form of ministry to others through her stress on contrition. Early in her narrative, she visits a monastery where a wicked monk at first despises her (ch. 12), but then asks her if she can tell him in what ways he has most displeased God. She promises to weep on his behalf, and 'wept wondrously for his sins', after which God reveals to her that the monk has sinned principally in lechery with married women, in despair, and in hanging on to wordly goods. When Margery confronts him, she counsels him, 'Grieve for your sin, and I shall help you to grieve'; she also urges him to confess his sins and give up his high office within the monastery. On a return visit some time later, she finds that he has undergone a complete conversion of life.

Similarly, towards the end of her *Book*, we see Margery being actually asked to weep for individuals as they lie on their deathbeds. The text comments rather wrily:

> Also, the said creature was desired by many people to be with them at their dying and to pray for them, for, though they had no love for her weeping and her shouting in their lifetime, yet they wanted her to both weep and shout when they came to die, and so she did.

This whole strand of weeping for others receives its clearest confirmation while Margery is in Rome. There, kneeling one day in the church of Santa Maria Maggiore, where the body of St Jerome was reputed to lie buried, she sees a vision of this saint, who says to her: 'Blessed are you, daughter, in the weeping that you do for the people's sins, for through it many shall be saved.' (ch. 41). And he assures her that she will be granted a 'well of tears' that shall never be taken from her.

There is a particular appropriateness in St Jerome appearing to her, as the Middle Ages regarded him as one of the major early Christian writers on the subject of repentance and tears. Although these themes emerge in nearly all Jerome's prolific letters and commentaries, perhaps their clearest statement comes in his letter to Rusticus.[1] Jerome wrote this letter to a husband who had resumed sexual relations with his wife after they had agreed to take a mutual vow of chastity. To exhort him to repentance, Jerome combed both the Old and the New Testaments for refer-

ences to weeping and tears, presenting a comprehensive
survey of the theme in Scripture. He drew heavily on the
psalms, and also pointed out that Christ himself wept, at
the tomb of Lazarus (John 11:35). Although Jerome provided virtually no commentary on these passages, this
comprehensive survey became a sort of handy short reference work on the topic for later generations. St Jerome's
appearance to Margery thus helps to establish her place in
an ancient and central Christian tradition of tears.[2]

However, although this weeping out of contrition already
caused adverse reactions among her neighbours, as we have
seen, it is the third strand, compassion for the suffering of
Christ, which seems to provoke the noisiest manifestations
in Margery – a form of bellowing that she herself calls
'roaring'. While her tears had very rapidly moved from just
contrition to a deep emotional response to anything connected with the life of Christ, it is the pilgrimage to the
actual scenes of Christ's sufferings which strongly develops
this aspect of her weeping. Her first real attack of crying
out occurs when visiting Mount Calvary in Jerusalem (ch.
28).

The whole of this chapter reflects a sequence of intense
emotions on Margery's part. First, on approaching Jerusalem, there is a feeling of joy and sweetness, so
overwhelming that she nearly falls off the donkey carrying
her. Then, the next day, as the Franciscan friars lead the
pilgrims on the standard procession round all the scenes of
the passion, she sees Christ in her soul 'verily by contemplation', and sobs and weeps as abundantly as if she had
seen his sufferings 'with her bodily eye'. Finally, on Mount
Calvary she falls to the ground, and 'wallows and wrestles'
with her body, stretching out her arms, and cries out with a
loud voice 'as though her heart would burst asunder'. She
cannot keep herself from 'crying and roaring even though

she might die of it'. She emphasises that this was 'the first cry that she ever cried in any contemplation', and that this experience repeated itself for many years after – as we saw in the chronology of her life, probably for a period of about ten years.

When she gets back to England, we see Margery undergoing a very similar episode one Good Friday, when she 'sobbed, roared, cried, and spreading wide her arms, said with a loud voice, I die, I die.' On this occasion a priest carried her out of the church into the cloister, thinking she needed air (ch. 57).

This strand of Margery's weeping is closely allied to her equally intense feelings when she receives communion. When she spends six months in Rome on her return journey from the Holy Land, she asks Christ for a 'well of tears', wherewith to receive his body with devotion (ch. 32). Again, back in England, we find that her cries on receiving communion necessitate special arrangements for her: the Dominicans give her communion in their private chapel, with two men having sometimes to support her until her cries had ceased. When this arrangement was later stopped, she received communion in her own parish church of St Margaret's, her cries being audible right round the church and even in the street outside (ch. 57).

It is probably this extreme manifestation that startles modern readers and has earned Margery the label 'hysterical'. Yet, at the time, although her neighbours were disapproving and branded her a hypocrite, accusing her of putting it all on, by and large the church authorities seem to have understood and accepted this behaviour. In some ways this is the reverse of what one might expect: modern critics seem to assume that it was the local people who were naive enough to be impressed by her screaming, while the church authorities tried to suppress this over-dramatic conduct.

When we look at the late medieval tradition of weeping, we can see why this form of behaviour would not necessarily have been shocking to Margery's more informed, widely experienced contemporaries.

As we saw, the tradition of tears in the Western Church goes back at least to St Jerome, and many of the scriptural texts he assembled were given a prominent place in the liturgy for Lent, the great season of repentance.[3] The desirability of actual tears of repentance was further emphasised in the votive Mass 'Pro peticione lacrimarum', which could be offered specifically to ask for the gift of tears. Its prayers include petitions that God will 'draw forth from the hardness of our hearts tears of compunction, that we may be enabled to weep for our sins'; 'produce from our eyes an abundance of tears'; 'grant us compunction of heart for our sins and rivers of tears'.[4]

In the Christian East, this tradition found one of its strongest and best-known statements in 'Step 7' of *The Ladder of Divine Ascent* by St John Climacus. This Greek text was written in the late sixth or early seventh century, by a deeply revered monk who spent forty years as a hermit before becoming abbot of St Catherine's monastery on Mount Sinai. It makes some bold claims for the value of tears. While commenting that we have all defiled the baptism we received in childhood, John Climacus asserts that the sins committed after baptism are washed away by tears; he even implies that these tears are essential to salvation: 'If God in his love for the human race had not given us tears, those being saved would be few indeed and hard to find.'[5]

This text circulated in Latin in the late Middle Ages, [6] and may have influenced a text much closer to Margery: Walter Hilton's *Ladder of Perfection*, which we are twice told (chs 17 and 58) was read to Margery over a number of years, along with other spiritual works. Hilton maps out with extraordinary closeness the pattern of Margery's weeping, during the course of two short chapters (Book I, chs 34–5).[7] At the start of someone's conversion, he says, a person thinks a great deal about his or her sins, with great fits of weeping, and this continues however often they go to confession. This leads on to meditation on the passion, which is given to the soul as a consoling gift by God. Hilton describes this contemplation as a feeling that one is seeing in one's soul the Lord in bodily likeness, as though he were on earth, and seeing him go through the various steps of the passion – very much as Margery describes when she is in Jerusalem. Hilton phrases the meditator's response to these scenes as follows: the heart is stirred to such great compassion for Jesus 'that you mourn and weep and cry with all the powers of your body and of your soul'. Hilton's generally serene style masks the fact that to 'cry' with 'all the powers of the body' could quite easily describe a reaction as extreme as Margery's on Mount Calvary.

This possibility is enhanced by the fact that Margery's own priest-scribe tells us (ch. 62) that he was won over to an acceptance of her conduct by reading a similar phrase in the text *Stimulus Amoris*, ascribed to St Bonaventure: the text describes how the lover of God acts madly, so that passers-by comment, 'Look, that mad man cries in the streets'. Although the passage is appropriate to Margery when one thinks about it in the light of her conduct, it would be easy to miss the fact that it is talking about shouting aloud, if one were reading it in a vacuum. Once alerted to the literalness of medieval 'crying', however, it becomes clear that many of the late medieval spiritual classics talk about this extreme behaviour. Margery's scribe, for instance, goes on to refer to Richard Rolle's *Incendium Amoris* (*The Fire of Love*), another of the texts which she lists as being read to her.[8]

If we had only the deceptive mildness of the spiritual classics to refer to, we might be tempted to think that Margery's scribe was erroneously applying them to her condition. But we also have several lived examples of this kind of behaviour, recorded for the most part in the lives of saints and visionaries. Margery's scribe describes one such life at some length: that of Marie d'Oignies, who was born at some point in the late twelfth century and died in 1213. He does not mention that, like Margery, she was a married woman who persuaded her husband to agree to sexual abstinence,[9] but he stresses the fact that she wept tears of compassion whenever she thought about the Lord's sufferings, and that she also incurred the enmity of priests whose services she disrupted with her sobbing and cries (ch. 62).

Another example, which may not have been known to either Margery or her scribe, shows some particularly interesting parallels to Margery's experience: that of Angela of Foligno, a thirteenth-century Franciscan tertiary.[10] Angela was a married woman, with children, who seems to have been born around 1248, and to have belonged, like Margery, to the rich merchant classes. She too has a priest-scribe (this time writing in Latin), who begins his narrative with Angela's conversion in 1285, when she is thirty-seven years old. Like Margery, before her conversion she was proud and fiery and particularly concerned with showing off in rich clothes. Her conversion begins when she is at last able to confess a mortal sin, never specified, which had previously nearly brought her to despair: her incomplete confessions had convinced Angela that she was receiving communion sacrilegiously. Her desperation drives her to pray to St Francis to send her a discerning confessor; he appears to her in a dream, and the very next day, she finds one.

After confessing fully, she embarks, like Margery, on a life of prayer and penance. Her acute sense of sin finds its only consolation in the ability to weep. She desires a life of sexual abstinence, and also, far more strongly than Margery, she feels that her mother, her husband and her children are great obstacles in her path to God. Consequently, she has no hesitation in praying for them all to die. Sure enough, in a short space of time they all do so, and, says the text: 'Because I had taken up the aforesaid spiritual path, and because I had asked God that they should die, I then indeed had great consolation from their deaths.'[11] Neither Angela nor her scribe makes the slightest comment on this brisk attitude to family relationships. In comparison, Margery's silence about her children could almost rank as maternal warmth.

Angela now has increasingly frequent visions of Christ on the cross, and experiences violent ecstasies; if she heard anyone speak of God, she says, she screamed (*'stridebam'*). Like Margery in Rome, she is driven to give away the bulk of her possessions to the poor, and wishes to become a Franciscan tertiary, that is, a member of the order while continuing to live in her own home. The Franciscans are at first reluctant to admit her, because her screaming is controversial: as with Margery, people think she is physically or mentally ill, or, more seriously, *'demoniata'* – possessed. However, in 1291, when she is about forty-three, they relent.

She then goes on pilgrimage to Assisi, and here has a spectacular attack of screaming.[12] On the journey, she had been overwhelmed by the sense of the presence of God, and on entering the lower basilica at Assisi, feels a sense of unendurable sadness at the thought that she might lose this presence. She begins to scream and grind her teeth, and falls to the ground. The friars come running from all quarters to see who is causing this disturbance, among them her confessor, who happens to be staying there at the time. He is so embarrassed and outraged at her behaviour that he forbids her ever to come near Assisi again. However, it is this confessor who eventually is so impressed by her that he becomes her scribe, despite opposition from other members of his order.

There are other similarities to Margery: she lives out the rest of her life in her home town, and she also experiences a spiritual marriage to the Godhead. However, she seems to have been widely revered towards the end of her life, with a circle of disciples able to record some of her discourses, so that we have material on Angela from far more sources than we have for Margery.[13] She died in 1309, at about the age of sixty.

Similar examples have been explored by Margery's modern defenders, such as Katherine Cholmeley in 1947, Edward Watkin in 1953, and Clarissa Atkinson in 1983.[14] Between them they make it clear that Margery is but one example of a well-known form of spirituality in the late Middle Ages. However, there is one aspect of Margery's experience of weeping and screaming which seems to be particularly developed in her case.

As we saw, both Marie d'Oignies and Angela of Foligno caused disruption in church by their uncontrollable sobbing, but in their case they seem to have been profoundly embarrassed by the public nature of their weeping, and have seen nothing positive in their disruptiveness. Margery is also acutely embarrassed, but Christ exhorts her to accept her effect on others as an integral and important strand in her particular vocation. In a sequence of two important chapters (chs 77–8), he talks to her at length about why he will not take her disturbing cries from her, although she implores him to:

> You see how the planets are obedient to my will, so that sometimes there come great cracks of thunder, which terrify the people. And sometimes, daughter, you see how I send great bolts of lightning, which burn down churches and houses. And sometimes you see that I send great winds which blow down steeples and houses and uproot trees from the ground, and do much damage in many places, and yet the wind cannot be seen, but it may well be felt. Right so, daughter, do I act with the power of my Godhead: it cannot be seen by men's eyes, but it may well be felt in a simple soul in which it pleases me to work my grace, as I do in yours.

After stating that he has set Margery on fire with love as though by lightning, he goes on with the long analogy of natural disasters:

> And sometimes, daughter, I make earthquakes in order to strike fear into the people, so that they should dread me. And this, daughter, is what I have done with you spiritually, and with other chosen souls who are to be saved, for I turn the earth of their hearts upside down and terrify them, so that they fear that vengeance will fall upon them for their sins.

One of Margery's functions, he explains, is to be an example to other sinners, so that they might know that whatever they have done, they need not fall into despair. In chapter 78, Christ elaborates on this function:

> I have ordained you to be a mirror among them, having great sorrow, so that they might learn from your example to have some little sorrow in their hearts for their sins, so that through it they may be saved; but they do not like to hear of sorrow or contrition.

Margery, then, has been appointed as a sign to others,

first of the power of God, in the way that lightning, storms and earthquakes can be such signs; then as a mirror, in which others can see reflected the repentance that should be within themselves.

In the context of the debate about Margery's personality, what are we to make of this? This appointment as a 'sign' could indeed be the ultimate example of Margery's preoccupation with her own standing in the eyes of others. On the other hand, it could be that, in an age in which the story of Christ had become all too familiar, it was indeed her task to remind everyone of just how 'earth-shaking' that story was meant to be.

One final incident illustrates this function. To a priest who, finding her sobbing before a crucifix (ch. 60), says to her, 'Woman, Jesus is long since dead', she replies: 'His death is as fresh to me as if he had died this same day, and so, I think, it ought to be to you and to all Christian people.'

Five

JOURNEYS

WE HAVE now surveyed the material which usually gives rise to the first set of charges against Margery, that her spiritual experiences arise from madness or hysteria. As we have seen, she and her contemporaries were quite clear that there was a difference between psychotic episodes and mystical experiences. Further, the weeping and screaming which have led modern critics to dub her hysterical were part of a well-recognised pattern of late medieval devotion. Of course, modern readers might well find this whole pattern of devotion dubious in itself, but, as the last chapter showed, it is described in major medieval writers, such as Hilton, normally respected for their calmness and good sense. There remained the problem of Margery's personality, which, as we saw, strikes many people as self-advertising and insensitive to the reactions of others.

This problematic personality perhaps also lies behind the second major charge against her, which we will now examine: that through claiming to be a mystic, she engineered a more exciting life for herself than was otherwise open to her.

MARGERY'S 'EXCITING' LIFE

This exciting life is characterised by several journeys, both abroad and within England, and by her repeated arrests and trials for heresy. While anyone might like to travel widely, probably only a person with a somewhat unhealthy taste for drama in her life would want to engineer repeated arrests which, Margery knew all too well, could end in her being burnt at the stake. As we saw in Chapter 3, a former parish priest of hers, William Sawtre, was the first man in England to be burnt for Lollardy. Nonetheless, the idea that a woman of Margery's obvious energy might be driven to find an outlet for her drive and restlessness – any outlet, however dangerous – has found an echo with modern readers, particularly among feminists.

However, it is increasingly becoming clear that someone of Margery's substantial merchant background, in a fifteenth-century town, had considerable scope for their energies. Before looking at Margery's journeys and trials, therefore, it is worth surveying her general situation as a middle-class secular woman.

First of all, it is evident throughout the book that Margery has control of her own considerable financial resources. Apart from setting up two businesses of her own, she also paid off her husband's debts, at his request, before leaving for the Holy Land. The fact that he has to ask her to do this, and has no automatic access to her funds, shows how much more autonomous medieval women were financially than, for instance, their Victorian counterparts, whose money seems mostly to have passed into the control of their husbands on marriage. In addition, she herself financed her first long journey abroad, which lasted eighteen months, during which she had to support herself without recourse to any form of casual employment on the journey itself. This must have required an outlay commensurate with that of a similar lengthy period abroad today.

Secondly, there is nothing of the 'cottage industry' about Margery's two ventures into business. Her brewery, she tells us, was for some years one of the largest in Lynn, which was, at that time, a busy port, with interests associated with nearby Norwich, at that time one of England's most populous towns. Indeed, it is intriguing that one of the references in the town records to a John Kempe, apparently Margery's husband, describes him as a brewer, as though on the official level his activities have been absorbed into hers. We do not in fact know what John Kempe himself did for a living, but his father is described in the records as a skinner. This skinning business seems to have been on a considerable scale, endowing his father with enough wealth to engage three ships to export his goods, and to engage in a claim for damages against the government of Prussia.[1] John, who seems to have been the second son, perhaps assisted his father in the skinning business.

Margery's own family seems to have been of higher standing than her husband's. Her father, John Brunham, was several times elected Mayor of King's Lynn, and twice one of its two Members of Parliament. He was then the Alderman of Lynn's Guild of the Holy Trinity, the most powerful of the town's guilds, which in effect elected the Mayor.[2] As John Brunham's daughter, Margery seems to have been known far beyond her home town, as we see when the Bishop of Worcester summons her to an informal meeting purely because he knows her family (ch. 45).

Apart from these indications of wealth and social standing, Margery seems to have had in John Kempe the model of a supportive husband, who never placed any restriction upon her. As we saw in Chapter 2, when she recovered from her bout of insanity he commanded that the household keys be restored to her, against the advice of everyone around her. Later, he never seems to object to any of her enterprises or journeys, and later still he frequently accompanies her, thus lending her important protection and respectability. Most self-sacrificingly of all, he eventually agrees to the lifelong cessation of their sexual relationship.

With money of her own, a prestigious background, and freedom to pursue her own interests, Margery's opportunities compare well with those of a woman with independent resources in our own day. There were of course, absolute barriers to the overt participation of women in public life, but nothing in Margery's narrative suggests that she felt frustration in this area. When describing her former proud conduct, she talks about flaunting expensive clothes, not about trying to influence the decisions of the powerful men in Lynn.

If, after all the above, a life of pilgrimage seemed preferable, this could have been practised by Margery without any claim to mystical experiences. Her recovery from insanity would have furnished adequate grounds for a particularly devout life, as she herself indicates when she says that she began to go to shrines in England 'inasmuch as she was cured' (ch. 10). Recovery from illness was the main motive for going on pilgrimage, according to Chaucer: people went to Canterbury to give thanks to St Thomas Becket, who had helped them 'whan that they were seeke'.[3]

In any case, pilgrimage was so widely practised in medieval life, by all classes of society, that there was no need to claim any special reason for choosing to travel in this way, and certainly not any need to display piety above the norm. This is demonstrated not only by Chaucer's fictional pilgrims – amongst whom is the rumbustious Wife of Bath, who has been, she claims, three times to Jerusalem – but also by Margery's own fellow travellers on her various journeys.

Those who are kind to her, such as Richard the humpback and Margaret Florentine, come across as ordinary men and women of goodwill, with no particular pretensions to holiness. Those who are unkind to her, like the profane louts who travel with her to the Holy Land, show that a completely irreligious cast of mind was no bar to this kind of adventure: according to Margery, her fellow pilgrims were annoyed with her for speaking about the Gospel, and furious that she would not eat meat like the rest of them. In fact, Margery would have had altogether an easier and pleasanter time had she been more ordinary.

THE FOREIGN JOURNEYS

So let us turn to the journeys abroad. As we saw in the chronology of her life, Margery made three journeys: one of about eighteen months to Jerusalem and Rome; one of a few weeks to Compostela in Spain; and, near the end of her life, another journey of about three months, when she visits shrines in northern Germany.

Of these journeys, the first, being both the longest and the one which took her furthest afield, into other climates and cultures, is the one which we tend to scrutinise most closely for Margery's reactions to new sights and sounds. It is also the one about which she tells us most, since it contained for her several crucial developments in her religious life, among them the beginning of her screaming in prayer and her spiritual marriage to the Godhead. Nonetheless, as pointed out in the chronology of Margery's life, the disappointing aspect of even this journey in her narrative is that we are told so little about the actual places she visits. As to her other journeys, she tells us nothing at all about Compostela, and on her third trip, understandably enough since she is now about sixty years old, she is chiefly preoccupied with the dangers and physical hardships of travel.

We therefore have to reconstruct what Margery would have experienced from other medieval writers. We will concentrate on Margery's first and most important journey, since, by good fortune, quite a few accounts of medieval pilgrimages to the Holy Land survive. Two come down to us from the fourteenth century, of which the more important one, that of Burchard of Mount Syon, was heavily drawn on by the writers of the fifteenth century, from whom thirteen accounts have come down to us.[4] All this material has been usefully collated into one general description of a medieval journey to the Holy Land by Hilda F. M. Prescott in her book *Jerusalem Journey*.[5]

The most immediately striking aspect of these accounts is that, for the most part, we find that Margery is not alone in her lack of descriptions. Just as modern 'autobiography', as a form of literature, was in its infancy, with Margery nowadays hailed as its first practitioner in English, so too was 'travel writing'. Among the writings surveyed by Hilda Prescott, only one work shows the kind of curiosity we might expect, and consequently she draws heavily on this one account: that of the Dominican friar Felix Fabri, a Swiss, who went to the Holy Land in 1480 and 1483. An earlier account is also of some interest in relation to Margery: that of the English priest William Wey, who went to the Holy Land in 1458 and 1462. He has the further advantage of having also written about his trip to Santiago de Compostela, where Margery went on her second journey abroad, and which he visited in 1456.

WILLIAM WEY'S *ITINERARIES*

William Wey illustrates well the kinds of information we get, and fail to get, from a medieval travel account. Wey was one of the first Fellows of Eton College, which had been founded by King Henry VI in 1442. He was given special permission by the king to absent himself from his college duties in order to go on his pilgrimages, and later in his life he became an Augustinian monk.[6]

In describing his first journey to the Holy Land, he disappointingly says nothing about his route from England to Venice; however he appends a list of the towns in Belgium, Germany and Lombardy through which pilgrims should expect to pass, and this allows us to reconstruct the route he probably took. Instead, Wey begins with useful information about exchange rates between the different currencies which would be encountered on the way, such as the ducat, noble and guilder, and he then gives instructions on what provisions the pilgrims need to buy in Venice. For example, they will need to buy their own bedding for the sea voyage, which can be sold back at half price on their return.

His account goes on to list the places visited in a standard fourteen-day tour of the Holy Land: Jaffa, Ramle, Lydda, Jerusalem, Bethlehem, Mt Judea, Jerusalem again, the river Jordan, Bethany; then back the way they had come through Jerusalem, Ramle and Jaffa. This list is then followed by a sort of gazetteer, in which the description of each site is extremely brief and factual. About the only point at which he allows himself to dilate on his material is when he introduces disparaging remarks about the other branches of Christianity encountered in Jerusalem, where most pilgrims would have met non-Roman Catholics – such as Eastern Orthodox and Monophysite Christians – for the first time. For example, he says of the Nestorians that they gave rise

to Mahomet.[7] This gazetteer is followed by Wey's narrative
proper, but this again is short on descriptive detail, and is
chiefly useful for indicating how long the journey could be
expected to take. Thus we discover that the journey from
England to the Holy Land took nine and a half months; of
these, four weeks and four days (18 May – 18 June) were
spent at sea, on the voyage from Venice to the port of Jaffa,
the only place at which the Muslim rulers of Palestine would
allow the Christian pilgrims to disembark.

In his account of his second journey,[8] he allows himself
to say more about some of the striking places he visited or
ceremonies he attended, but these turn out to be mostly in
Europe. This time he spent a month in Venice, at this period
perhaps the most exotic and glittering European port. He
was fortunate in arriving in the city in time for St Mark's
Day, the patronal festival of the Cathedral; he saw the funeral
of the recently deceased Doge; he also witnessed the annual
ceremony of Venice's marriage to the sea. On this second
journey, the sea voyage to the Holy Land took six weeks.
However, he does not tell us much more about the Holy
Land itself. On his return, he spent time in Rome, and
describes the churches there. For example, he tells us about
the notable relics in St Maria Maggiore, which was believed
to hold the complete bodies of the Evangelists Matthew and
Luke, and of St Jerome, and, as well as a piece of the true
cross, the cloth and hay on which Christ lay in his crib.[9]
These details illustrate the kind of 'description' that we
get in Wey's account: most of it takes the form of further
information. It is not visually descriptive, nor does it consist
of compellingly narrated incidents. Consequently, we do not
really form a picture of what it might have felt like to go on
such a journey, at such a time in history.

Wey's account of his journey to Compostela shares the
same problem. Although it was his first pilgrimage, he keeps

his account of it until last.[10] He tells us that he travelled in a company of six ships, which set out on 17 May 1456 from several different ports in England: Bristol, Plymouth, Weymouth and Lymington. This is useful information in relation to Margery, for, as we shall see, she tells us that when a ship could not be obtained in Bristol, many pilgrims tried their luck in other ports; this detail indicates which ones she probably had in mind.

The sea journey to Corunna took four days, and Wey reached Compostela in time for a major feast-day, Trinity Sunday. And what does he tell us about this great centre of pilgrimage? He lists the number and rank of the clergy in the Trinity Sunday procession; he lists some of the major gifts made to the shrine; he informs us of the indulgences to be gained by going on this pilgrimage. These are pieces of somewhat clerical information which might have conveyed something of the grandeur of Compostela to other church officials, but do not perhaps convey a great deal to us. The only colourful detail about his time in Spain is his noting down of a four-line verse that the local urchins sang as they begged for money, while performing acrobatics before the pilgrims. Of the journey, the only detail he gives is to note another couplet, this time in English, about the terror that every seafarer feels on passing the Lizard on the dangerous Cornish coast.

As we can see, Wey is chiefly concerned to provide useful, practical information of the briefest sort. In relation to Margery, the main function of accounts such as his is to confirm or throw light on some of the details she gives us about her own journey. We deduce from these other accounts that it was normal to embark at Venice, as she did. The group of pilgrims she is with spends thirteen weeks there, which seems a bit long, but engaging a ship might have been more difficult than they expected. From the other pilgrimage accounts it appears that the sea journey was made almost exclusively in spring and high summer, between April and August, and every ship plying the route must have been booked up. Margery mentions the group eventually hiring a ship and buying bedding, and she then buys bedding of her own. God warns her against embarking on the particular galley that has been hired, and on her advice, several pilgrims join her on another galley, first selling off the barrels of wine they had already paid for on the first ship (chs 27–8). This ties in with what the other accounts tell us about the pilgrims needing to buy all their own provisions for the sea journey while still in Venice.

Knowing the set tour outlined by Wey, we can also make sense of Margery's movements during her three weeks in the Holy Land, as when she refers to a trip to the river Jordan, and to passing through Ramle on her way back from Jerusalem. As was pointed out in the chronology of her life, about the only 'foreign' detail she gives us about her time in the Holy Land is when a handsome Saracen helped her up the mount of Christ's temptation, known as 'Mount Quarentyne', near Jericho. William Wey twice stresses the height of this mountain, once in the English prologue to his work, and again in Latin within the main text.[11] He is particularly careful to stress the difficulty of the ascent of Mount Quarentyne in the English prologue: 'It is passing hot and right high'. He advises pilgrims to rest after coming back down the mountain, before eating only a little food and drinking a little wine; they must on no account drink water as this may cause fever. In the light of Wey's remarks, it becomes less surprising that Margery should choose to mention this particular incident in her journey, rather than another. This arduous climb must have stood out in her memory, and the refusal of her fellow pilgrims to help her must have caused her real difficulty. The help of the Saracen would have been all the more necessary and welcome.

A comment by William Wey also throws light on a particular phrase used by Margery: her description of Christ's crucified body, which she beholds in contemplation while on Mount Calvary, as being 'more full of wounds than ever a dove-house was of holes' (ch. 28). As we saw in Chapter 1, this particular phrase has been fastened on as an example of the literary shaping of Margery's account by the priest-scribe, who might here have been drawing on a metaphor found in the writings of St Bernard. Chapter 1 points out that this metaphor is widely used in more popular writings as well, but Wey's account suggests an underlying source for all these references. Calvary, a fifteen-foot mound, was enclosed within the same building which housed, in another corner, the Chapel of the Holy Sepulchre. The distinctive feature of this chapel was its round roof 'made like a dove-cote', says Wey, and covered with lead.[12] Is it not possible that the dovecote analogy was a standard one made to all pilgrims by the Franciscan guides, who explained to them the significance of each site? Margery herself tells us, in the Calvary chapter, that 'the friars always, as they went about, told them what Our Lord suffered in every place'.

Her stay in Rome during her journey back also finds support in some of the details provided by Wey. As mentioned above, he lists the body of St Jerome among the relics in St Maria Maggiore, and, as we saw in the last chapter, Margery had an important vision of St Jerome while kneeling in this church.

In general, the other pilgrimage accounts help us to see that the very few details given by Margery are probably not arbitrary or random, but represent the most memorable highlights of her trip, which would have been recognised as such by other pilgrims of her day. The fact that there are

so few highlights can most likely be explained by the passage
of time: she is, after all, recalling them at least fifteen years
after the event.

FELIX FABRI'S *EVAGATORIUM*

We have to turn to Felix Fabri to get anything like a modern
travel account, in which the personality of the traveller is
allowed to shine through, bringing with it shamelessly sub-
jective comments about the places visited, and a frank
indulgence of curiosity for its own sake.

Felix's account stands out from the others of this period
by being a deliberately humorous and colourful record of
his personal experiences. To begin with, it is a much longer
work: it covers not only his travels in the Holy Land, but
further journeys into Egypt and Arabia as well.[13] This greater
scope allows him to relate the kind of incidents we might
expect to find in Margery Kempe's account. Thus, when the
pilgrims, after about five weeks at sea, first catch sight of
the mountains of the Holy Land, we can share in their awe.
Felix describes the way the look-out's cry brings everyone
running from all parts of the ship, and when they all burst
into singing the Te Deum, the sea rings with their voices –
not least because, although everyone is pronouncing the
same words, the pilgrims all sing in the slightly different
notations of their respective countries, producing,
according to Felix, a strangely beautiful dissonance. The din
is further enhanced when every musical instrument to be
found on the ship is brought on deck and played. For
three days the pilgrims see only mountain-tops until they
eventually come in sight of Jaffa, and they have to content
themselves with recognising the holiest mountains, such as
Mount Carmel, where the prophet Elisha lived as a hermit,
and the mountain where the Maccabees lie buried.[14]

It is incidents like this that draw us into the slow pace of travel of the medieval world, and allow us to appreciate the concomitantly long, slow build-up of excitement and desire in the pilgrims themselves. After landing at Jaffa, they had a ride of at least two days over hilly country to get to Jerusalem. No wonder Margery tells us that, at her first sight of the city, she nearly fell off her donkey for joy. Can she have been the only one to be so intensely moved?

This brings us to one of the most useful aspects of these other pilgrimage accounts in relation to Margery. They allow us to gain some perspective on how her extreme responses struck her fellow pilgrims, and indeed on whether these responses were that far out of the ordinary.

If we remember that Margery 'roared', fell to the ground and 'wrestled' with her body at Mount Calvary (enclosed, as we saw, in the same building that housed the Chapel of the Holy Sepulchre), Felix's account of the conduct of his fellow pilgrims on first entering the courtyard before the Holy Sepulchre is extraordinarily pertinent. In the case of his large and rather sophisticated group, they had been obliged, by various bureaucratic difficulties, to spend nine days after landing at Jaffa before they could proceed to Jerusalem. For them too the entry into the holy city had been a moving event, but the outburst of emotion at the Holy Sepulchre was so astonishing that Felix describes it at length.[15]

The pilgrims flung themselves down and kissed the earth many times. One would have witnessed, he says, such abundant tears, such bitter and heart-felt groans, such sighs, laments and sobs, that even a heart of stone would have burst into tears with the pilgrims. More relevantly to Margery, some pilgrims fell to the ground and lay there, as though bereft of strength. Some were prostrate for so long, they seemed dead. Others knelt, opening their arms in the form of a cross, while others wandered around beating their breast. Others were shaken by such violent sobs that they were unable to stand, and had to sit down, clutching their heads.

As to the sounds that were uttered, apart from the general sobbing engaged in by all, Felix draws attention to the shrieks of the women. They screamed as though in labour, he says. It seems as though Margery would simply have been doing what many others would have done. In fact, one wonders if she experienced her 'first great crying' in Jerusalem precisely because similar sounds would have been uttered all around her.

Modern medicine might recognise in the scene described by Felix the signs of mass hysteria, and it may well be that there was something hysterical about this shared emotion. Its compulsive aspect is suggested by Felix when he says of those wandering around that they moved as though 'driven by an evil spirit'. However, there may also be an element that is culturally conditioned in this behaviour, particularly in that of the women. An article by H. P. Weissman draws attention to artistic and literary representations of the 'compassion' of the Virgin Mary, watching her son die as she stands at the foot of the cross. Weissman quotes, among other texts: ' . . . she wax oute of here mynde; / She swouned, she pyned, she wax half dede, / She fylle to the grounde, and beete her hede.'[16] That Margery might have been influenced by such representations when she was on Mount Calvary is suggested by her own words, where she says that just before she uttered her first roar: 'Before her face she heard and saw in her spiritual sight the mourning of Our Lady, of St John and Mary Magdalen, and of many others that loved Our Lord.' (ch. 28).

Whatever the cultural pressures on the pilgrims, not all the members of the group were affected in the same way. Felix himself speaks as a detached observer, without going so far as to criticise those who show these strong emotions. However, some, he tells us, were so unaffected as to laugh at the behaviour of those around them. Far from sharing their spirit of cynicism, Felix has severe censure for these mockers. They held the more devout pilgrims to be 'fools, hypocrites, vain-glorious, deceivers and brain-sick', a list of insults which corresponds with surprising closeness to some of the adverse judgements passed on Margery in our own day. Felix says roundly of the mockers that they were 'brutish men, blind to all piety, void of all religious feeling, full of all uncleanness'. Although he himself does not participate in the mass hysteria, if that is what it is, he respects the piety behind it.

Felix's account explains why there seems to be no astonishment on the part of Margery's fellow pilgrims when she falls to the ground and roars in Jerusalem. The puzzled responses described in the chapter which records her first 'cry' all belong to the 'many years after' in which this roaring and shouting continued after she returned home. Margery's priest-scribe adds a further comment of his own, pointing out that people cry out and conduct themselves in the same way over the loss of an earthly friend or relative, or even over a great material loss: a useful reminder to us that, in any case, Margery belonged to a far more demonstrative and emotionally expressive age than our own.

In conclusion, what we learn from other medieval accounts of journeys to the Holy Land is that Margery's rather flat and spare description, when closely compared with them, stands up surprisingly well. These other narratives, with the exception of Felix Fabri's, are no more colourful in terms of foreigners encountered and places visited than hers is. What they do give us is fuller information, whereby we can see that Margery's pilgrimage appears generally to accord with standard practice. More importantly, they help us to see the rationale behind the few details that she does give: these seem to belong to the agreed high points of a Holy Land pilgrimage, and not to be a meaningless selection. As we saw, her conduct can also be seen in relation to that of other pilgrims, and emerges as less eccentric and difficult to believe than modern readers might at first expect.

It is important to establish Margery's credibility in relation to her pilgrimages, because, as we shall see in the next chapter, one of the charges made against her at her heresy trials was that she never went on them. The sketchiness of her accounts – as we saw, she says nothing at all about Compostela – might at first lend some weight to such a charge. Closer examination of the journeys, however, allows us to see, rather, that Margery is simply using extreme economy in getting through the narrative of her life, the primary focus of which is her inner development and not her outer adventures. As mentioned in the chronology of her life, she herself, or perhaps her priest-scribe, makes this focus her somewhat dry defence in connection with her third journey: 'She gave her mind more to contemplation than to the names of the places' (Book II, ch. 4).

Six

TRIALS FOR HERESY

WE NOW turn to the second element in the charge that, by posing as a mystic, Margery engineered for herself a more exciting and dramatic life: her repeated arrests and trials for heresy.

At first glance, we might get the impression that Margery's manner of life was deliberately provocative, and that she thus brought the trials on herself; or that the fault lay with the Church authorities, who are assumed to disapprove of mystical experience in a lay person, particularly in a woman. However, as we saw when establishing the chronology of Margery's life, it is important to look at the proportions, in terms of time, of each set of events within her overall narrative. In particular, we need to take note of the timing of the heresy trials.

As we saw, Margery landed at Bristol after her journey to Compostela in 1417, and decided not to go straight home but to visit her spiritual advisers in York. On her way there, she was arrested at Leicester, then twice questioned at York (first by the Cathedral Chapter, then by the Archbishop), before being rearrested and brought before the Archbishop again at Beverley; she was stopped again at Hull, but this time released; a short time later, after her return home, she and her husband were stopped at Ely, but again released (chs 46–55). As we established in the chronology, all these arrests take place within a few weeks of each other, mostly between August and October 1417. It is important to realise that Margery was not subjected to harassment throughout her life, being arrested regularly at, say, three- or four-year intervals. Instead, all the trials for heresy cluster together within one extremely short space of time. If we look at the historical events of 1417, an explanation for this spate of arrests begins to emerge.

THE OLDCASTLE REBELLION

Within Margery's text, it is the trial at Beverley which points us beyond purely religious considerations and suggests a link with the political situation of the moment. One of the charges thrown at her at Beverley is that she is 'Cobham's daughter' and 'sent to bear letters about the country' (ch. 54). As Windeatt points out, this probably meant 'spiritual daughter', that is, follower and disciple, of Lord Cobham, better known as Sir John Oldcastle (1378–1417), one of the leading Lollards of the day. Oldcastle had married Joan de la Pole, the heiress of the Cobham lands, and had thus become 'Lord Cobham' on his marriage.[1] At this point in time, the Lollard movement had entered its most political and violent phase.[2]

The name 'Lollard', a pejorative term originally meaning 'mumbler', had become rather loosely attached to any persons holding opinions similar to those espoused by the Oxford philosopher and theologian John Wycliffe (c.1329–84), during the last eight years of his life. Wycliffe left his teaching post at Oxford in 1374, when he was forty-five, and withdrew to a country living at Lutterworth (midway between Coventry and Market Harborough), accompanied by a few close disciples and friends. From there he launched several works attacking, among other things, the authority of the clergy and the doctrine of the Real Presence in the Eucharist, and strongly espousing the doctrine of predestination. It is no wonder that later Protestants regarded him as a pre-Reformation hero and forerunner.

Apart from Wycliffe's immediate disciples at Lutterworth, early Lollards seem to have consisted of a few strictly localised groups: in 1382, we find a group of secular clerks (clergy not belonging to religious or monastic orders) at Oxford; and a group of laymen and unbeneficed clergy at Leicester. From there, the Lollard influence seems to have spread to the surrounding Midland areas. The first repressive measures against the Lollards were taken at this time by the Bishop of Lincoln, John Buckingham, in whose enormous diocese both Leicester and Oxford lay. As a result, some Lollards took refuge in the dioceses of Worcester and Hereford, and in the South Wales marches. This area thus became a stronghold of Lollardy, particularly the port of Bristol, one of its busiest towns. Bisected by the river Avon, which here formed the boundary between the dioceses of Worcester and Wells, Bristol found itself relatively unmolested by either of its two bishops.

From 1382 to the end of the fourteenth century, Lollardy seems to have spread quietly among the laity of the artisan and smallholder classes, who seem to have looked to the knightly class for leadership. Sir John Oldcastle, whose own family lands lay in Herefordshire, was typical of this class, advancing his family fortunes by successfully serving the king as an energetic soldier. However, most of the Lollard knights seem to have returned to an orthodox doctrinal position, at least in public, after 1401, when the act *De Heretico Comburendo*, allowing the burning of heretics, was promulgated. Oldcastle seems to have been unusual in sticking doggedly to his position.

At first, this did not prevent him from becoming a trusted servant of Henry IV, who seized the throne, deposing the devoutly orthodox Richard II, in 1399. Nor did it prevent him becoming a close friend of the king's heir, the young Prince Hal, as readers of Shakespeare will be aware: Old-castle was the original version of Falstaff's name, and it was pressure from the outraged descendents of the real Oldcastle, who considered that a great Protestant martyr was being traduced, which forced Shakespeare into hastily changing the name of his most rollicking character.

It is possible that at this stage no one in authority realised just how heretical Oldcastle's opinions were. However, 1410 finds him writing warmly to Jan Hus and other leaders of the similar heretical movement in Bohemia. It is likely that the authorities had their eye on him from that moment.

In March 1413, Henry V succeeded to the throne, and Oldcastle was immediately arraigned as 'the principal har-bourer, promoter, protector and defender' of Lollards, particularly on his own lands in Herefordshire, and on the scattered Cobham estates he had inherited by marriage, which lay around London and in Kent. Chief among these estates was Cooling Castle, in the marshes north-east of Rochester. It seems that Henry was reluctant to prosecute his old friend, but Oldcastle was eventually summonsed in August that year. Despite at first barricading himself into Cooling Castle, he was captured, brought to trial, and con-demned to death on 25 September. However, Henry decreed a forty-day delay before his execution, hoping that he would recant. During this delay, Oldcastle escaped from the Tower of London on 19 October, and spent the next two months in hiding near the capital, planning an uprising aimed at destroying the new king.

Even in 1413, there may have been some impingement of Oldcastle's plotting on Margery's life. It is not clear at exactly what point after her conversion she went to Canterbury (ch. 13), but the visit seems to come after she had made her vow of celibacy with John Kempe on Midsummer Eve, 23 June 1413 (ch. 11). Her being reviled by the monks, and threatened with burning by the crowd to cries of 'false Lollard!', becomes more comprehensible against the background of Oldcastle's imprisonment, trial and escape in that same period. After his escape, in particular, the authorities were aware of his plotting and were already moving to pre-empt a possible uprising.

Fortunately for Margery, she seems to have left England later in 1413, on the first stretch of her journey to the Holy Land. She was thus safely out of the country when Oldcastle's plotting bore fruit in the major Lollard uprising of January 1414. The uprising was immediately put down, but Oldcastle escaped arrest and went on living in hiding, mostly, according to rumour, in the vicinity of his lands in Herefordshire.

The interest of this 1414 rising, in relation to Margery, lies in what emerged about its organisation, during the trials of those involved. Apparently, insurgents made ready to rise in each county. Their organisers, lay people, mostly weavers, led by local chaplains, were to let Oldcastle's supporters know at what point they would arrive in London, arrange quarters there, and generally act as channels of communication between the London plotters and those in the provinces, particularly in Derby and Bristol. In fact, Bristol furnished the largest single contingent of insurgents. It seems likely, therefore, that when we come to the events of 1417, the authorities were trying to uncover a similar network of messages being carried about the country: hence the charge that Margery was 'carrying letters for Cobham', a charge made all the more plausible because she was coming from the direction of Bristol, near Oldcastle's estates.

A second important outcome of the 1414 rebellion was the enactment of a statute in April that year, enabling the secular authorities to work more closely with the Church in putting down the Lollard movement. As a consequence of the attempt on the king's life, Lollardy was now not only a matter of heresy but also of treason. Hereafter, we find the secular arm not only acting in its traditional role of executioner *after* an ecclesiastical trial had been held, but also bearing the prime responsibility for hunting down and arresting Lollards in the first place. This secular persecution turned out to be more sustained and co-ordinated than the previous sporadic attempts to suppress Lollardy, which had been carried out by individual bishops within their own dioceses.

As we have seen in previous chapters, Margery's journey to the Holy Land and her prolonged stay in Rome on the way back lasted about eighteen months or a bit more, and she seems to have returned to England just before Trinity Sunday 1415, which that year fell on 26 May.[3] Just at this period, Oldcastle was associated with a second attempt to destroy the king, the 'Southampton plot' of 1415. Henry V was about to set sail on his first expedition to France, and this plot aimed to take advantage of the king's absence by destabilising the country: the Scots were to invade the north of England, while Oldcastle was to provide a similar disturbance in the west by calling on his Welsh ally, Owen Glendower. The king was on his way to embark at Southampton in July that year, when news of the plot was brought to him, enabling him to suppress it before it could be put into effect. Although the Southampton plot failed, the overall plan for stirring up trouble in the king's absence was not abandoned.

When Henry V sailed for France in June 1417, on his second expedition to claim the French crown, Oldcastle made his final attempt against the king. The uprising began with the Scots crossing the border in mid August 1417, and besieging the towns of Berwick and Roxburgh. Henry had appointed one of his younger brothers, the Duke of Bedford, as Lieutenant of the kingdom, responsible for its security during his absence. The Duke of Bedford hastened north to fight off the Scots' attack, supported by the Archbishop of York. This explains the Duke's presence in the north at the time of Margery's trial at Beverley, and the officious zeal of his retainers. In the meantime, rumours of Oldcastle's movements had increased, particularly in the Midlands. On 15 July 1417, he was reputedly sighted in Northamptonshire; in response, a commission was set up on 22 July to investigate Lollard sentiment in the Midland area.

Now where was Margery in 1417? That year, as we saw in the chronology of her life, she went on pilgrimage to Santiago de Compostela. After scraping the necessary funds together in Lynn, she arrived in Bristol on 'Wednesday in Whitsun week', which would probably have fallen near the beginning of June.[4] This journey was obviously planned long before, as Margery tells us that she had arranged with Richard the humpback, while still on her previous journey abroad, to meet him in Bristol two years after her return, so that she could repay him some money he had lent her. She was thus somewhat caught out by events, for, after a successful rendezvous with Richard, she had to wait six weeks in Bristol for a passage to Spain, as all English ships had been requisitioned by the king to carry his troops across to France. The dearth of ships is illustrated by her comment that other pilgrims went from port to port looking for an available passage, but were eventually forced to return and wait in Bristol (ch. 44). She must have embarked, then, about the middle of July, and she was away, in all, twenty-six days (ch. 45). This brings us approximately to mid August 1417, when the Scots had just invaded the north of England.

It seems likely, then, that Margery was just one person caught up in the general political panic caused by the Scots' incursion of August 1417, as she made her way northwards from Brisol to York. Because of this incursion, the hunt for Oldcastle was on, and anyone travelling about the country could be suspected of being a Lollard messenger. In particular, she seems to have walked straight into the arms of the commission looking for Lollard sympathisers in the Midlands. It is significant that it is at Leicester, long regarded as the Lollard capital, that Margery was first molested, having left Bristol and travelled via the shrine of the Holy Blood at the Cistercian Abbey of Hailes, in Gloucestershire, without incident. She then meets trouble at York, and, again significantly, is picked up by the Duke of Bedford's men and retried at Beverley.

Bedford finally succeeded in capturing Oldcastle late in 1417, and had him executed in London on 14 December that year. No leader among the insurgents emerged to take Oldcastle's place, and his execution thus brought this violent phase of Lollardy, with its accompanying highly organised persecution, to an end.

This context makes far more sense of some of the details of Margery's trials, which come to us, as did the details of her travels, through the selective economy of her memory. As with her pilgrimages, the trials are significant events to Margery in so far as they represent inner developments in her spiritual life; she is not interested in external whys and wherefores, which she makes no effort to explain, or indeed to comprehend, as far as we can tell. However, one of the details that emerges from the trials is that the greatest animosity against her comes from the secular authorities, not the Church, as we might expect if it was genuinely her spirituality which was under scrutiny. In the light of the historical developments mapped out above, let us see if we can find a coherent rationale behind Margery's repeated arrests.

MARGERY'S TRIAL AT LEICESTER

As we have seen, she was tried for the first time at Leicester, where it is the Mayor who suddenly has her seized, puts her under house-arrest and imprisons her two male companions. He accuses her of Lollardy, and arranges for her to be tried before the ecclesiatical authorities. While she is awaiting this trial, she is pulled out of her place of imprisonment and brought before another secular officer, the Steward of the Earl of Leicester.

This turns into a bizarre encounter with two equally unpleasant and perplexing phases. In the first, the Steward interrogates her in the presence of a number of priests. He addresses her first in Latin, which she makes clear she cannot understand; he then asks her 'many questions' in English, which she successfully answers. The content of the questions is not specified, and the attendant priests seem to be present merely as witnesses. In the second phase, the Steward, 'a handsome man' (ch. 47), takes her into a separate room, uses obscene language and gestures towards her, and grapples with her physically with such force that she is convinced she is about to be raped. He finally desists, 'astonished', when she tells him her revelations are from the Holy Ghost.

If the Steward initially thought that Margery was some kind of secret agent, his desisting on finding that her motivation was genuinely religious might seem less abrupt.

Admittedly, a less likely secret agent than Margery, with her conspicuous clothing and behaviour, it is hard to imagine. In Leicester, she had already caused a sensation by her loud weeping before a crucifix in a local church, and when the Mayor arrested her he was especially suspicious of her white clothes. However, using her to carry letters might have been thought of as a particularly cunning stroke, and the Steward's addressing her in Latin (which happens nowhere else), surrounded by many clerks, might have been a way of estimating how sophisticated a person he was dealing with.

Margery was finally brought before the ecclesiastical authorities some days later, in the persons of the Abbot of Leicester and the Dean of one of Leicester's two collegiate churches of St Mary. This ecclesiastical trial proceeds in an orderly manner, with Margery being questioned systematically about the articles of her faith, beginning with what she believed about the Eucharist. The Abbot and the Dean are 'well pleased' with her answers (ch. 48), but the Mayor, who is present, continues to be suspicious of her. He insists that she obtain a letter from the Bishop of Lincoln 'by the which the Mayor should be excused', discharging him from any responsibility for her. It is significant that it is the Mayor, the secular authority present, who feels accountable for letting Margery continue her journey, rather than the Abbot and the Dean, who in fact become good friends of Margery and subsequently show her much kindness and hospitality.

THE TRIAL AT YORK

Finally set free in Leicester, after being delayed three weeks, Margery gets to York on 'Our Lady's eve', presumably the day before the Nativity of the Virgin Mary, that is, on 7 September. She stays in the city for two weeks before she is tried again. Initially, she is summoned to appear voluntarily before a gathering of clerics in York Minster's chapter house. The questioning as to the articles of her faith proceeds routinely, and she appears to pass the test with complete success. Nonetheless, she is summoned to appear before the Archbishop some days later in his palace at Cawood, ten miles south-west of the city. This time her appearance is not voluntary, and she narrowly escapes being remanded in prison until the date set for trial.

Margery's trial before the Archbishop is one of the great scenes of her *Book* (ch. 52). Many of the bystanders call her 'Lollard' and 'heretic' as she awaits the Archbishop's entrance. She is shaking with terror, and as she prays for help she bursts out into loud shouting and sobbing. As a result, her trial opens with the Archbishop asking her roughly, 'Why are you crying like this?' To which she answers, 'Sir, you will wish one day that you had cried as bitterly as I.'

She again gets through the questioning on the articles of faith successfully, and the Archbishop seems prepared to acknowledge her innocence. However, he asks his assistants, 'What shall I do with her?', a question which may have been prompted by the tense political situation. In other words, he seems to be asking for advice on whether or not to let her go. Some clerical enemies that Margery has made in York during her two-week stay continue to malign her; after further stormy scenes, the Archbishop makes Margery promise to leave his diocese, and pays one of his men to escort her out of it.

Margery does not leave the diocese immediately. She first goes eastwards to Bridlington, on the coast, and continues to experience hostility along the way. Eventually, she travels south to the Humber, the boundary of the diocese, and is about to cross it by boat when she is arrested by the Duke of Bedford's men. They tell her that the Duke is looking for

her, on the grounds that she is held to be the greatest
Lollard in the area and in the region around London – a
reference, perhaps, to Oldcastle's Cobham estates around
London and Rochester. The men hope for a reward of a
hundred pounds (an enormous sum at that time) for capturing her, and drag her off to Beverley (ch. 53).

It so happens that the Archbishop is there, and so it falls
to him to investigate her case yet again. Clearly wishing to
be rid of her, he staunchly defends her orthodoxy, and it is
at this point that Bedford's men bring their charge that she
is one of Cobham's followers and is carrying letters for
him. Furthermore, they accuse her of not having gone on
pilgrimage to Jerusalem and the Holy Land (ch. 54).

This charge could be a religious one, in that Lollards
disapproved of pilgrimages, so that having been to the Holy
Land would be a strong sign of orthodox belief and
devotion. However, uttered by these secular accusers,
immediately after the charge that she is carrying letters, the
accusation is more likely to be a political one: that she was
not out of the country, as she claimed, during the crucial
period of the 1414 uprising. The Archbishop dismisses these
charges as slanders, but a Dominican friar, who is one of
the Duke of Bedford's party, maintains that Bedford is determined to seize her. It is interesting that the Archbishop
responds that he does not want to incur Bedford's anger on
her account, implying that the secular authority very much
has the upper hand in this matter. However, he succeeds in
getting Bedford's party to agree to his sending her once
more out of his diocese, on condition that she goes to
London to obtain a letter attesting her orthodoxy from the
Archbishop of Canterbury, in whose province she normally
resides.

Although Margery is stopped twice more and generally
harassed by the authorities on her way home, this is the last

of her actual trials for heresy. Her leaving the dangerous north may account for this.

THE CHURCH'S ATTITUDE TO MARGERY

What emerges from the trials is that no one who examined Margery seriously doubted her orthodoxy, or seems to have been troubled by her crying and general spirituality. In each case, she wins over the ecclesiastical authorities. Although she does have persistent traducers among some of the clerical bystanders, several of these apologise to her in private (e.g. chs 51 and 52), and give the impression that they publicly take a hard line against her in order to keep themselves from adverse notice or criticism. Possibly, the tense political climate made it dangerous for most clerics to react to anyone suspected of Lollardy with anything other than a show of horror. However, although Margery is officially cleared of any error whatsoever, this does not mean that the Church is necessarily comfortable with her life-style.

Several areas of unease emerge during the course of the trials. One is her apparent independence of her husband: one of the questions asked her in the chapter house of York Minster, for instance, is whether she has her husband's permission to come to York. Further, one of the charges made against her at Beverley is that she encouraged a woman of the aristocracy, Lady Westmorland, to leave her husband, which Margery vigorously denies. It is possible to see here a purely mundane fear that Margery will have a subversive effect on the conventions governing the behaviour of married women. Even well-wishers among the laity urge her to stay at home and spend her time spinning as other women do, rather than bringing such discomfort and anguish upon herself (ch. 53). Noteworthy here is the enmity of other women: when Margery is arrested

by the Duke of Bedford's men, women come running out
of their houses with their distaffs, crying that she should be
burnt. This reaction suggests that Margery has touched a
deep anxiety in women as well as men.

The second area which most riles individual clerics is the
teaching dimension of Margery's calling. At both York and
Beverley, criticism is made of certain stories she is reputed
to have told, particularly against the clergy. When pressed
for details. Margery retells moral fables or short parable-
like 'exempla', which the Archbishop seems to find both
impressive and amusing. However, at the end of her trial at
Cawood, he tries to make her promise not to teach people
within his diocese. This she refuses to do, on the grounds
that everyone may speak of God. Margery is on dangerous
territory here, in that lay preaching and teaching was a
feature of Lollardy, and moreover she supports her argument by quoting from the Gospel. Since the Lollards
maintained the supreme authority of Scripture over any
teaching authority of the clergy, this compounds the danger.
Not surprisingly, the clerics present exclaim, 'Now we know
well that she has a devil within her, for she speaks of the
Gospel!' – a line of wonderful narrative irony.

The whole subject of her telling 'stories' might have been
raised as part of the investigation into her religious position.
But a certain animus in this matter seems to emerge in the
trials, which goes beyond the anxieties of the moment about
uncovering Lollards. The fact that Margery's ministry
involved her in frequently rebuking people, particularly
clerics, for profane language and lives of gross self-indulgence seems to have made her something of a thorn in the
flesh to rank-and-file clergy. On Margery's side, or that of
her scribe, something of this animus is replicated: there is
no disguising the glee with which the text depicts this
untutored lay-woman getting the better in argument of her

clerical detractors. We are told, for instance, that when she was released from Cawood, she was received in York by many friends who rejoiced that God had given her, an unlearned person – 'not lettered' – wit and wisdom with which to answer so many learned men successfully (ch. 52, end). On her way home, in Lincoln, she answers those who revile her with such wisdom and effectiveness that people marvelled at her 'cunning', that is, knowledge and skill. Even some lawyers, normally held to be the supreme practitioners of skilled argument, are envious, saying that after many years of study they cannot answer as she does, and asking her where her 'cunning' comes from; to which she replies that it comes from the Holy Spirit (ch. 55).

However, whatever the element of rivalry here between Margery and certain clergy, no one argues that she does not have a right to rebuke sinful language and conduct whenever she comes across them, and no steps are taken to try to suppress this side of her ministry.

Her screaming, prayers and visions are nowhere adversely commented on. The one aspect of her spiritual life that does cause her a lot of trouble with the authorities is her wearing of white clothes. As we saw, this annoyed the Mayor at Leicester, and Margery insists on explaining the matter privately to the Abbot and Dean. Again, at York, the Archbishop asks her why she wears white clothes, adding, 'Are you a virgin?'. This question suggests that the clothes were recognised primarily as a sign of chastity, and not, as some critics have suggested, as indicating that Margery was suspected of belonging to one of the more extreme movements within the medieval Church, such as the Flagellants, who also wore white.[5] However, once again, no one tries to stop her wearing this garb.

One other area of unease emerges from these trials: the simple fact that she had evidently become rather famous,

or at least notorious. Not only do the Duke of Bedford's
men maintain that the Duke is specifically on the look-out
for her, but when Margery gets to York from Leicester, the
anchoress whom she had gone to York to see refuses to
receive her, because she has heard so much slanderous talk
about her (ch. 50). At her trials in York and Beverley, there
is constant reference by those present to tales that are circu-
lating concerning her person, her words and her conduct.
Her sheer notoriety seems to have made her something of
a headache to the authorities.

Nonetheless, it would be a mistake to view Margery's
repeated trials for heresy as an attack by the Church authorities launched specifically and consciously at her as an
individual. Rather, as we have seen above, the political events
of 1417 suggest that Margery was simply one person among
many who must have been caught up in the general turmoil
caused by the threat to the kingdom that summer. The trials
occupied only a few weeks of Margery's life, and were not
repeated.

Where does this leave the charge that Margery, by claiming
to be a mystic, engineered a more exciting and dramatic
life for herself than was otherwise open to her? As we saw
in the last chapter, Margery could have gone on pilgrimage
without any claim to being more than usually devout, and
have conducted herself with her characteristic intensity
without arousing undue comment. Then, as we saw in this
chapter, her trials for heresy were probably not launched
specifically against her, but befell her as part of the specific
political situation obtaining during a brief period of the
year 1417. It is true that Margery cannot be seen purely as
a hapless victim, selected at random: her notoriety, her white
clothing and her screaming would be bound to attract the
attention of the authorities in a time of national danger,

when they had a duty to arrest anyone acting suspiciously. However, it is the contention of this chapter that, had it not been for the particular events of 1417, Margery might well have spent her whole life without being brought to trial. In that case, a lot of the apparent drama of her life disappears.

Seven

VISIONS

WE CAN now turn to the third set of charges against
Margery: that, although she may be a genuinely devout
woman, her 'visions' and 'conversations' with Christ are flat
and unconvincing, are somewhat suspect for being largely
concerned with herself, and have no message in them of
value to others.

The visions and conversations present us with slightly different problems, so we will examine them separately. If we
take the visions first, most readers would probably agree
that there is a qualitative difference between her first vision
of Christ, when she is miraculously healed (ch. 1), and all
the other experiences that she appears to report to us as
'visions'.

This first vision comes to her unexpectedly and unbidden.
Christ appears, clad in a purple robe, and sits on the edge
of her bed. There is something spontaneous and unexpected about this action, which gives the vision its sense of
independent life. Christ then asks a single question:
'Daughter, why have you forsaken me, when I never forsook
you?' This terseness contrasts with the prolixity of all Margery's subsequent conversations with Christ. He then slowly
ascends before her eyes, thus bringing this brief experience,
which seems to have lasted only a few moments, to an
end. Again, this is in marked contrast to the length and

elaborateness of most of her other visions. Most important of all, this first vision has momentous consequences for Margery, in that it brings about her instantaneous and complete restoration to sanity. It thus escapes the somewhat casual and pointless impression given by some of the other visions.

These later visionary experiences not only lack the spontaneous and unexpected quality of the first, but tend to fall into well-defined sequences. The first major sequence, described soon after Margery's conversion, begins with the birth and childhood of the Virgin Mary, proceeds to the events surrounding the nativity of Christ, and ends with the flight into Egypt (chs 6–7). The second takes place while Margery is in Jerusalem, and focuses, as one might expect, on the sufferings of Christ on the cross (chs 28–9). The third sequence, which is recounted when Margery is back in Lynn, goes over the events of the passion again, but this time within the context of their liturgical re-enactment, from Holy Thursday to the morning of Easter Day. These events are then followed by Christ's ascension into heaven and the death of the Virgin (chs 73, 78–81).

In fact, these scenes can be said to follow an orderly progression through the life of the Virgin Mary, which itself encloses an equally orderly progression through the major events of Christ's earthly life. They suggest, in short, a series of meditative exercises. Why, then, does Margery not straightforwardly call them this? To find a possible answer, we need to look at the way the first sequence of visions is introduced.

After her conversion, she spent a few years living an intensely prayerful and ascetic life, followed by a period of near despair, as we saw in the chronology of her life. Margery then experienced a breakthrough when Christ 'ravished' her soul. As part of the new set of instructions that he gives her for the next stage in her life, Christ tells her to stop saying a great many prayers – 'leave your bidding of many beads' – and, instead, 'think such thoughts as I will put in your mind' (ch. 5). She is allowed to say whatever prayers she wants to until 6 am, but after that she is to 'lie still' and speak to God 'by thought'; and, he goes on, 'I shall give to you high meditation and true contemplation'. He then instructs her to go to a particular Dominican anchorite for counsel in this new enterprise. The anchorite tells her that she is 'sucking even at Christ's breast', and he charges her to 'receive such thoughts when God will give them' with great humility, and to report their content back to him for reassurance as to whether these thoughts really come from God.

After this careful preparation, we find Margery attempting to put this new approach into effect (ch. 6). When the time comes for her to meditate, she 'lay still, not knowing what she could best think'. She asks Christ for help: 'Jesu, what shall I think?' He immediately responds that Margery should think about the Virgin Mary; and 'at once she saw' the Virgin's mother, St Anne, great with child, and she begs St Anne to let her be her servant. The vision continues with unbroken momentum from that point.

What is emphasised throughout this account is that this kind of meditation is a new departure for Margery, pin-pointable in time; more than that, it represents the crossing of a threshold, from reliance on vocal prayer to using the mind, specifically the visual imagination. Secondly, the crossing of this threshold is not a self-chosen act. The meditations begin not only at God's command, but in response to his gift: both Margery and the Dominican anchorite emphasise the passive, receptive nature of her role in this new form of prayer. This includes the intimation that the thoughts will come in God's good time, not hers: she is to

receive the thoughts 'when God will give them'. Walter
Hilton, describing this kind of meditation, also emphasises
its received quality: 'One cannot have this kind of meditation at will, but only when our Lord wills to give it.'[1] For
Margery, then, 'high meditation' is not an activity within
her control, but a new and rather daunting experience
which she is to dispose herself to receive.

When we come to the content of the first meditation, it
is the visual aspect that is emphasised: 'She saw St Anne
great with child.' Indeed, it is the awakening of the visual
imagination which seems to mark Margery's crossing over
from vocal to mental prayer. However, this awakening
appears to be distinguished from the series of vision-like
dreams which she experienced soon after her conversion,
although she does not record them until near the end of
the *Book* (ch. 85): in one she sees a child-angel in white,
holding the Book of Life, in which her name is written; in
another, she sees Christ as an extremely handsome man,
lying down, while someone comes and cuts open his breast;
in a third, she is aware of Christ standing just above her,
and takes his toes in her hands so that she actually feels the
flesh and bones; in yet another, she sees the Virgin Mary
gently wrap the infant Christ in a white cloth. All these
visions come to her while she is kneeling in church, yet in
a light sleep, or sleep-like trance: 'her eyes kept closing as
though she wanted to sleep'; 'suddenly she was in a kind of
sleep'; 'her eye-lids half closed as in a kind of sleep'.

These 'dreams' or 'trance-visions', if we can call them
that, all occurred before Margery went to Jerusalem.
Chronologically, there may have been some overlap with the
beginning of her 'true contemplation', particularly as this
last dream suggests a thematic link with the first sequence of
meditative visions. However, the 'dreams' differ from these
meditations in an important respect: there is a genuinely

unsought and random quality about them, plus a delicacy and momentary evanescence, through which we can guess at the almost breathless hush with which Margery must have received them. Finally, they left behind them 'a new spiritual joy' and sense of comfort too wonderful for her ever to manage to express.

In contrast, although Margery experiences her meditations as a gift that she passively receives, rather than as an exercise she actively controls, she obviously feels required to put a little more conscious effort into them than into the 'trance-visions', which come upon her almost in spite of herself, against her efforts to stay awake. This would account for her being at a loss when it comes to embarking on her first meditation: she does not know 'what she could best think'; she does not know what she is meant to do.

This somewhat ambiguous passive/active character of the meditations may account for the similarly ambiguous language with which she usually introduces them: 'she saw', 'she saw in her contemplation', 'she went forth in her contemplation', 'it seemed to her spiritual sight', 'she beheld in the sight of her soul', 'she thought truly that she saw our Lord appear . . .'. Interestingly, 'appear', used by itself without any preceding 'she thought', seems to be confined to the first healing vision and to the dream-visions. However, the general impression given by the meditations is that, once she has embarked on them, they take on a visual life of their own, so that she seems to be reporting them to us as events, in the same way that her first healing vision was an event.

However, even if the reader resists thinking of the meditations as visions and classifies them as exercises, their subject-matter remains somewhat problematic for modern readers. The first sequence, beginning with the birth and childhood of the Virgin Mary, illustrates the problem well.

Margery has no sooner 'seen' a figure such as St Anne, or the Virgin herself, or the Christ-child, than she enters into self-preoccupied conversation with them, or at least tells us what her own actions were within the scene. Thus she takes charge of the child Mary and feeds her 'with good food and drink' until she is twelve years of age. Similarly, she begs for white cloths in which to wrap the infant Christ when he is born, and procures bedding and food for both him and his mother. These gestures of service have their own sweet, if rather prosaic, charm, but their sheer domestic pragmatism, unaccompanied by any thoughts on the significance of the events, is one of the elements which gives these 'visions' a slightly pointless feel, quite apart from the fact that Margery herself occupies centre stage for much of the time.

However, the aspect which perhaps most causes something of a recoil among modern readers is the repeated praise for Margery uttered within the vision. Thus, once Mary has conceived, Margery falls on her knees and says, 'I am not worthy, Lady, to serve you.' 'Yes, you are, daughter,' Mary replies, 'follow me, for your service pleases me well.' They go together to visit Elizabeth, and stay with her until the birth of John the Baptist. On taking their leave, Margery begs Elizabeth to ask Mary if she can continue to serve her. 'It seems to me, daughter,' Elizabeth replies, 'that you carry out your duties very well.' (ch. 6).

There are, in contrast, some touching moments in these scenes, which show Margery's particular brand of devotion at its best. For example, when she swaddles the infant Christ, she says to him, 'Lord, I shall handle you carefully; I shall not bind you too tight; be not displeased with me.' And when she sees the three kings, for once she doesn't enter into conversation with them, but merely bursts into tears when they leave, unable to bear the thought of them going away from Christ's presence. For Margery, the thought of anyone's separation from Christ, however legitimate its cause, is an agony.

How are we to account for Margery's retelling of 'visions' which, in general, seem so pedestrian and so self-preoccupied? The meditative tradition in which she was working may enable us to perceive what could be of value in them.

The use of the visual imagination, which plays a key role in what she recounts, was strongly encouraged throughout the late Middle Ages.[2] In fact, its value was recognised even in the succeeding age of the Renaissance, and was formalised, for example, by St Ignatius of Loyola, the founder of the Jesuit Order, in his *Spiritual Exercises* as 'composition of place'. In this exercise, the imagination is used not just to picture a scene from the Gospels in one's mind, but to make it as real and as present as possible, so that one is not so much observing the scene as reliving it.[3]

This form of meditation was extremely popular in Margery's day, and many detailed descriptions of the key scenes from the life of Christ were circulated, in both Latin and English, as an aid to this kind of visualisation. Margery's description of the scourging of Christ, for example, reflects the standard way in which this scene was imagined at the time, with Christ tied to a pillar with his hands above his head (ch. 80). Similarly, the description of Christ's body being pulled taut by ropes when he is being nailed to the cross is also widespread in the literature of this period; perhaps the best-known example occurs in the York mystery play of the crucifixion.[4]

The most influential of these texts was probably the *Meditationes Vitae Christi*,[5] attributed in the Middle Ages to the Franciscan friar St Bonaventure. This author is twice listed by Margery among the spiritual writers whose works were read to her, and this could have been one of the texts she was referring to (chs 17, 58). Although modern scholarship no longer ascribes the *Meditationes* to St Bonaventure, they do typify the whole tradition of Franciscan spirituality at this time, with its heavy emphasis on the human vulnerability and suffering of Christ. Mention has already been made of Richard Rolle's *Meditations on the Passion*, which Margery might have been familiar with: although she specifically mentions only the *Incendium Amoris* among Rolle's works (chs 17, 58), she goes on to say that 'other such' works were read to her.

The source that Margery herself explicitly acknowledges is what she calls 'Bride's book' (ch. 17), that is, the *Liber Celestis*, or *Revelations*, of St Bridget of Sweden, for whom Margery had a particular veneration. St Bridget (1303–73) had lived only a generation before her, dying just as Margery was probably being born, and during her stay in Rome Margery had met St Bridget's maidservant (ch. 39). It is easy to see why Margery would feel a strong affinity for this Swedish saint. She too had been a married woman, and had borne eight children, before she and her husband agreed to live chastely. After they had gone on pilgrimage together to Compostela, he joined a Cistercian community but died soon after, while she lived for a while as a hermit, before founding her own order, the Bridgettines. In 1349, Bridget went to Rome to gain the Pope's approval for her new order, and remained there for the rest of her life, serving the poor and sick. During this last period she also made a pilgrimage to the Holy Land.[6]

She had visions throughout her life, particularly of Christ's passion, which various priests who were her close friends recorded for her in the *Liber Celestis*. Of these revelations, Christ assures Margery, 'every word is true' (ch. 20), which suggests that Margery took Bridget's descriptions as particularly authoritative. In this work, the Virgin Mary herself guides Bridget through a fairly standard progression through the scenes of Christ's life. It has to be said, however, that Bridget's descriptions have more restraint than Margery's, although she is clearly working within the same broad tradition. In the scourging, for example, Margery specifies an outrageous number of blows, which she has got from some source other than Bridget.[7]

Most of these medieval visualisations of the life of Christ focus, as one might expect, on Christ himself and the other biblical figures surrounding him, and not on the meditator. Margery herself, in her later visions (such as the scourging and the crucifixion) is able to stand back and provide us simply with a vividly detailed description of Christ's sufferings. Nonetheless, her presence still intrudes at intervals. Thus, when Christ takes solemn leave of his mother on the eve of his passion, and she has fallen to the ground overcome by grief, Margery plucks at Christ's robe and demands to know what will become of her. He replies that he will return to comfort them both (ch. 79). Among other incidents, she is also strongly present when Christ is taken down from the cross (ch. 80), and at the death of the Virgin (ch. 73).

However, Margery's medieval audience may not have been as startled by these personal intrusions as we perhaps are. Within the medieval tradition of meditation, there is a more narrowly relevant strand, which has been carefully examined by Clarissa Atkinson. She examines the influential text *De Institutione Inclusarum* of Aelred of Rievaulx (1110–67), written in about 1160, when Aelred was already a leading Cistercian abbot. Purportedly the work was for the benefit of his sister, who was a recluse and had asked him for spiritual guidance in her chosen way of life, but from the outset it was taken as addressing a wider female audience. For example, the *Ancrene Wisse*, a thirteenth-century work for female recluses, acknowledges the influence of Aelred's work, and his text circulated in Margery's day in two English translations, one made in the fourteenth century and one in the fifteenth.[8]

Atkinson points out the closeness of Margery's nativity sequence to the corresponding scenes in Aelred.[9] In particular, the Cistercian abbot encourages his female audience not just to visualise the scene, but to insert themselves into it in much the same way that Margery does. Aelred was credited with bringing a softening effect to Cistercian austerity with his personal brand of gentle humanity, and we can see this at work in this text. The female meditator is encouraged to see herself as mingling with the other female figures in the life of Christ: thus she is to serve the Virgin Mary at the birth of Christ, and help to place him in the manger; she is to comfort Mary Magdalene in the garden, when she is grieved that she is not allowed to touch the risen Christ. In each case, the meditator is to practise humility by seeing herself only as a servant and helper.

This strand of meditation was also gathered up by Ignatius of Loyola, this time applied to both men and women. In his descriptive notes on the nativity, for example, he encourages the meditator to see himself present in the scene, and to make himself a poor, unworthy servant, ministering to the physical needs of Mary and Joseph with reverence.[10]

Apart from providing the opportunity to place oneself in a humble relationship to Christ, this putting of oneself into the scene has a further valuable dimension for the meditator: one's imaginary reactions can reveal hidden aspects of oneself. This psychological mechanism is perhaps best explained by a present-day Jesuit, Anthony de Mello, in his book *Sadhana*, which includes a modern application of the concept of 'composition of place'. He argues that the use of the visual imagination, which he terms 'fantasy', does not involve an idealised or compensatory view of ourselves as does daydreaming, but the projection of the true self, rather as do the dreams we receive in sleep: 'Fantasies, like dreams, are useful tools for learning about yourself because you project your true self into your fantasies.'[11]

We see this projection of the true, unidealised self at work in several places in Margery's contemplations. A particularly striking instance occurs late in the meditations, when she is visualising the death of the Virgin Mary (ch. 73). She pictures herself weeping so violently by the deathbed that the apostles, all of whom are also assembled round the bed, command her to be quiet. Unabashed, she responds, 'Would you that I should see the Mother of God die and that I should not weep?' There is perhaps an element of unconscious comedy here, which reflects Margery's lack of self-criticism in these scenes. On the other hand, her reproof to the disciples is not without its own dignity, which comes, perhaps, from the utter sincerity and depth of the grief that Margery is experiencing.

Both dignity and ludicrousness can coexist, as in her meditation on Christ's descent from the cross, where the very authenticity of her extreme behaviour gives the scene its own kind of sublimity. Here, Christ's body has been laid out on a marble slab; the Virgin Mary is weeping over his head, Mary Magdalen over his feet, and other Maries over each hand. This leaves no room for Margery, who sees herself running 'ever to and fro like a woman without reason, greatly desiring to have had the precious body to herself alone, so that she might have wept her fill in the presence of that precious body, for she thought she would have died with weeping and mourning at his death because of the love that she had for him.' (ch. 80). Here, the jealous possessiveness of her love, the brute force of her grief, are presented with a simplicity and directness which command respect.

A more innocuous instance of her self-projection is her

response to the homelessness of Mary and the child Jesus in Bethlehem, and later during the flight into Egypt: every night she rents lodging for them, which probably reflects the instincts of the wealthy woman that, at this point, she still is (chs 6, 7). More importantly, however, this is where we also see the valuable aspect of the domestic pragmatism referred to earlier. Margery probably was, in truth, a good practical housewife and mother, whose love for her children would have expressed itself largely through the humdrum tasks of keeping them clean, warm, fed and adequately sheltered. And why should she not also express her love for Christ in exactly the same way? One of the side-effects of late medieval spirituality, with its strong focus on the tenderness between Mary and the infant Jesus, was a lyricism in art and literature about the simple physical tasks of looking after a baby: wrapping him in swaddling clothes, feeding him at the breast, laying him in a manger, dandling him on one's knee. This is a genuinely innovative contribution from the medieval period to literary and artistic tradition; the classical age, which preceded it, has its sentimental moments about children, but not about the physical side of looking after babies.

In general, one could argue that medieval meditation on the home life of Mary, Joseph and the Christ-child had the effect of validating and, in a sense, consecrating domestic life for everyone. If we do not encounter more meditators like Margery, it is partly because so few of those who have left written records were lay-people at all, living in a domestic as opposed to a religious or monastic environment, and even fewer of them were women, who had actually wrapped up a new-born baby or worried about 'good food and drink' for a growing child. It is here that we can share the regret expressed at the beginning of Hope Emily Allen's letter to

The Times on discovering Margery's *Book*: ' . . . in the Middle Ages old ladies did not write their reminiscences.'

However, if Margery were simply projecting her own practicality into these scenes, we would surely merely appreciate their domestic charm, rather than retaining a strong sense of her self-preoccupation. To the extent that this kind of visualisation, with its accompanying projection of the true self, is a profoundly personal exercise, many people would probably feel instinctively that this kind of 'vision' was not to be shared, and would indeed be full of clumsy acts and embarrassing details which might be illuminating for the meditator, but not for anyone else. This is perhaps what lies behind the assertion of some critics that, while Margery was a genuinely devout and sincere woman, her visions and colloquies are largely concerned with herself, and have no message in them of value to others.

Why, then, does it not seem to occur either to Margery or to her priest-scribe to leave them out, or express any kind of reservation about them? We saw in the chapter on madness, for example, that Margery had great doubts about her prophetic gifts, and her priest-scribe is also sceptical enough to put them to the test (ch. 24). There is nothing comparable, however, in relation to the visions.

Anthony de Mello again provides a possible answer. He goes on to say that this kind of 'fantasy' can not only show you yourself, but can also change you. There is a sense in which intentionally visualised actions become real actions psychologically. Thus, to picture oneself serving the Christ-child is on one level actually to have performed this service. Margery's text bears this out: Christ assures her repeatedly that he will reward her for all the actions she has performed for him in contemplation just as though she had performed them in actual fact. For example, she tries to imagine dying for the sake of Christ, and with engaging honesty, tells us that her cowardice made her imagine the easiest death for herself, which she decides would be having her head struck off with an axe. Christ responds, 'I thank you, daughter, that you want to suffer death out of love for me, for as often as you think in this manner, you shall have the same reward in heaven as though you had suffered exactly that death.' (ch. 14). And near the end of the book he says:

> Also, daughter, I thank you for each and every time that you have bathed me in your soul at home in your own room, as though I had been present there in my humanity, for I know well, daughter, all the holy thoughts that you have shown towards me in your mind. And also, daughter, I thank you for all the times that you have lodged me and my blessed mother in your own bed. For these and for all the other good thoughts and good deeds that you have thought in my name and per-formed for my love, you shall have with me and with my mother, with my holy angels, with my apostles, with my martyrs, con-fessors and virgins, and with all my holy saints, all manner of joy and bliss everlasting, without end. (ch. 86).

For Margery, then, these meditations are important *events* within her spiritual life, actual steps by which she grows closer to God. They therefore need to be recorded in a truthful account of her life, as they occupy a central place in her development. Although Christ also thanks her for all the scorn and opprobrium she has endured for him in this life, which presumably includes her trials for heresy, it is not the trials or her journeys, or any other external event, which she presents as winning her a high reward in heaven, but these internal 'thoughts' in which she performed simple, practical services for the Christ-child.

As we saw, she also perceives these meditations as a gift which she receives, not primarily as an exercise within her control, and although during them she beholds Christ with her 'spiritual sight' rather than with her bodily eyes, she seems to feel that, once in progress, each meditation proceeds with a psychological life of its own which has, for her, an intense reality.

Eight

CONVERSATIONS WITH CHRIST

DESPITE THE questions raised by Margery's 'visions' or meditations, they are less problematic than the conversations with Christ, which actually form the bulk of the religious material in the book. There is some conversation with Christ, lengthy or brief, in almost every chapter of Margery's narrative.

ESTABLISHING THE NATURE OF THE 'CONVERSATIONS'

The sheer volume of this material causes a problem: in the New Testament and in later accounts by various mystics, the recorded utterances of Christ tend to have a powerful brevity. The single question that Margery records in her first healing vision, which brought about her full recovery of sanity, accords well with this tradition. Its earliest example is probably the conversion of St Paul, in which Christ asks one question, 'Why do you persecute me?' (Acts 9: 4–5).

Margery's second supernatural experience (fifteen years after the first), when she heard heavenly music, was similarly brief and powerful, in that it was this second experience which brought about her spiritual conversion. Her subsequent conversations with Christ, however, are lengthy, wordy, and for the most part have no particular consequences in her life.

She herself emphasises the somewhat chatty nature of God's 'dalliance' with her soul. As the word implies, dalliance is the kind of conversation that people engage in when they have the time and the familiarity to 'dally' together: leisured, expansive, ranging easily across a host of subjects from intimate and serious to light-hearted and trivial. Margery several times refers to God talking to her as to a friend (e.g. chs 17, 87):

> ... Oftentimes the Father of heaven dallied in her soul as clearly and truly as one friend speaks to another in bodily speech; sometimes the Second Person of the Trinity; sometimes all three Persons in Trinity and one Substance in Godhead dallied in her soul ... (ch. 17).

Katherine Cholmeley, considering this problem of verbosity in the 'conversations' of Margery Kempe, decided that these are genuine 'locutions', namely words of Christ heard mystically in the soul, and that it is Margery's acute memory which enables her to report them at such length.[1]

Unfortunately, perhaps the main problem with these interchanges is the disappointing first impression they give of monotony, lack of impact, and general absence of individuality in the purported utterances of Christ. As we saw in Chapter 1, Margery's first translator, Colonel William Butler-Bowdon, relegated most of the conversations to an Appendix, so little did he think them significant within Margery's main narrative. Furthermore, she herself perhaps dilutes their significance by mentioning that she also spoke to numerous other denizens of heaven, whose converse with her soul produced as intense a reaction in her as her conversations with God:

> Sometimes our Lady spoke to her mind. Sometimes St Peter, sometimes St Paul, sometimes St Katherine, or whatever saint in heaven she had a devotion to, appeared to her soul and

taught her how she ought to love our Lord and what she should
do to please him. Their dalliance was so sweet, so holy and so
devout, that this creature was often not able to bear it, but fell
down and wrestled with her body . . . (ch. 17).

In an almost identical passage towards the end of the *Book*,
she adds the names of St Mary Magdalen and St Margaret
to the list (ch. 87). In Rome, as we have seen, she experienced a vision of St Jerome (ch. 41), and, also in Rome,
when she could find no English-speaking priest to hear her
confession, St John the Evangelist stepped in and heard it
for her (ch. 32). For the most part, the words of the saints
are not recorded in the *Book*, but the few sentences that St
Jerome utters are indistinguishable in style from those of
Christ.

Several critics have commented on the standard 'clerical
voice' of these passages. Within Margery's book itself, the
discourse of the Carmelite friar William Southfield, whom
she visits in Norwich, is identical in general style, in tone
and rhythm, with the discourses of Christ (ch. 18).

Further, in one of Christ's own speeches, there is a sugges-
tive slip when, while commenting on a passage in the
Gospels, he refers to himself as 'our Lord' – 'where our
Lord says to his disciples . . .' (ch. 31), as though he were a
priest preaching a sermon. This slip is not a question of
some medieval convention, as one might at first suspect, but
also struck Margery's original readers: one of the medieval
annotators of the manuscript has here crossed out both 'our
Lord' and 'his', obviously expecting 'I' and 'my'.[2] Similarly,
Christ frequently commands her to do things 'in the name
of Jesus', where one might expect 'in my name'.

Apart from this generally clerical tone, the content of
some of the conversations sounds implausibly academic,
especially when compared to the vivid homeliness of many

of the visual 'contemplations' we considered in the last
chapter. For example, one long passage near the end of the
book sounds remarkably like Jesus rehearsing the Atha-
nasian creed:

> I know well enough, daughter, that you think you cannot
> worship the Father except you also worship the Son, nor can
> you worship the Son without also worshipping the Holy Ghost.
> And also you sometimes think, daughter, that the Father is
> almighty and all-knowing and is all grace and goodness, and
> you think the same of the Son, that he is almighty and all-
> knowing and all grace and goodness. And you think that the
> Holy Ghost has the same properties equally with the Father and
> the Son, since he proceeds from them both. Also you think
> that each of the three Persons of the Trinity possesses what
> the others possess in their Godhead, and so you believe truly,
> daughter, in your soul, that there are three distinct Persons and
> yet one God in substance, and that each one knows what the
> others know, and each one is able to do what the others are
> able to do, and each wills what the others will. (ch. 86).

How are we to account for the fact that Christ, St Jerome
and the earthly priest William Southfield, among others,
all use the same measured rhythms and balanced, rather
soporific tone? If there is intervention in the text from
Margery's priest-scribe, I suggest that it is in these passages
that it is perhaps to be detected.

First, some process of selecting passages for writing down
is implied by the text's repeated assertion that far more
conversations occurred than are recorded: 'It would be in
a way impossible to write all the holy thoughts, holy
speeches, and high revelations which our Lord showed to
her . . .' (ch. 59). Secondly, Margery herself says repeatedly
that she could never put into words her interchanges with
God, or the holy thoughts that accompanied her weeping:
'She had many a holy thought and many a holy desire which

she could never tell or repeat, nor could her tongue ever express the abundance of grace which she felt . . .' (ch. 78); 'She felt many a holy thought at that time which she could never tell afterwards' (ch. 73). Indeed, she says at one point that almost as soon as these interchanges were over, she could not even remember them:

> If one of her confessors came to her when she had just risen up from her contemplation or else from her meditation, she could have told him a great deal about the dalliance with which our Lord dallied in her soul, and yet within a short time afterwards she had forgotten the greatest part of it and nearly every item in it. (ch. 83).

Perhaps we have here the problem of a person whose verbal skills for expressing her intellectual perceptions have never been very much developed, which fits with what we might expect of someone more or less illiterate. Although in the Middle Ages to be illiterate was not necessarily to be uneducated or uninformed – we have seen how her parish priest read spiritual works to her (ch. 58), and she tells us that she gained her knowledge of Scripture from sermons and from conversations with clerics (ch. 14) – it is conceivable that she was not very articulate when it came to expressing the insights which she herself received. The verbalisation of her interchanges with Christ would, therefore, probably have to be fashioned on existing models.

The possibility of help from her priest-scribe in the matter of phrasing is perhaps hinted at when he says: 'With such kind of thoughts, and many more than I could ever write, she worshipped and glorified our Lord Jesus Christ for his holy visitation and for his comfort.' (ch. 87). The scribe's 'I' is quite startling here, as he does not use it casually like this elsewhere; when he introduces himself into the text, it is usually to comment at some length on his own initial scepticism towards Margery, as when he puts her prophetic gifts to the test (ch. 24), or when he describes how he ceased to be critical of her crying (ch. 62).

What, then, are the available models that Margery or her scribe might have used, consciously or otherwise? How widespread was the apparent experience of similar conversations at this period? Before we focus specifically on the late Middle Ages, it might be helpful to look briefly at the general tradition of hearing Christ speak and of having long interchanges with him.

When we explore this tradition, we find that we are not dealing with a central and widespread practice, supported by manuals of instruction, as we found with the use of the visual imagination in medieval 'contemplation'. Discussion by the great spiritual writers of the phenomenon of hearing words, as opposed to seeing images, does not seem to get under way until the sixteenth century, notably in the works of the two great Carmelite mystics, St Teresa of Avila and St John of the Cross.[3]

St Teresa considers the ways in which Christ speaks to the soul in her work *The Interior Castle*.[4] She distinguishes three different kinds of speech: (1) words heard outwardly with the physical ears, which she cannot comment on because she herself has never had this experience; (2) words which take shape in the imagination, which could come from good or evil spirits as well as from God; (3) words heard intimately in the soul, which are always brief, clear and full of meaning, are indelibly marked on the memory, and leave behind an immediate feeling of profound peace. It would seem that Margery's first vision of Christ, with its single question and its healing effect, would correspond to this last category, while the rest of her conversations might correspond to the second. The possibility that these 'words of Christ' could be inspired by spirits other than God might help to account for Margery's constant retelling of all her experiences to every possible spiritual adviser, to see 'if there were no deception in them'. Perhaps she herself is aware, even if she cannot articulate this, of the possible role of her imagination in what she is experiencing.

In *The Ascent of Mount Carmel*, St John of the Cross establishes a similar threefold division:[5] (1) the praying mind is used as an instrument by the Holy Spirit, and in a manner talks to itself, producing the impression of a conversation with God, partly through the earnest desire that most souls have to hear God; (2) 'formal words' can be heard, which are brief, occur unexpectedly, but have no particular effect on the person's life or character; (3) 'substantial words' are also brief and unexpected, but are engraved in the soul, and have an immediate and profound effect.

In St John's description, the hearing of lengthy conversations in the mind, while ultimately ascribed to inspiration from the Holy Spirit, is deemed to be a product of the mind itself. Since then, the issue of whether the actual phrasing in these conversations is to be taken as divine in any direct sense apparently remains unresolved. The encyclopaedic *Dictionnaire de Spiritualité* lists some twentieth-century examples of the genre, with this comment: the soul translates the illumination it receives into its personal language, and while the soul appears to be a passive recipient, it is free to rephrase the language on second thoughts, thus implying an active dimension.[6] Perhaps the 'active dimension' in Margery's case is an agreed co-operation with her scribe in the phrasing of these conversations.

St John has a further distinction to make. He maintains that all precisely discernible phenomena such as visions, revelations and words of God belong to the lower degree of contemplation, whereas confused, obscure, general apprehensions form the higher contemplation of naked faith.[7]

When Margery stresses the fact that she could never put
many of her 'thoughts' into words, and that often she could
not remember them, perhaps she is struggling to express
something akin to these 'obscure, general apprehensions'.
This possibility is occasionally suggested in the text: her
thoughts 'were so high above her physical senses that she
could never express them with her physical tongue exactly
as she felt them. She understood them better in her soul
than she could utter them' (ch. 83).

In this case, we can see the long, Athanasian-creed-style
discourse near the end of her *Book* as perhaps an attempt to
express in words the 'general apprehension' of Trinitarian
theology, as opposed to specific instructions for her own
life, that her contemplation eventually led her to. There is
something climactic about this particular discourse in the
book, as though we are being led with Margery through
the trials and tribulations of her spiritual life, to this sweep
of understanding near the end.

If, then, Margery and her scribe are striving to put words
to experiences which were basically inexpressible, where
would they have found other examples to follow?

MEDIEVAL MODELS OF 'CONVERSATIONS' WITH CHRIST

Margery was in fact not the first to recount this kind of
lengthy interchange. This form of devotional writing seems
to have developed largely during the fourteenth century,
and to be frequently associated with women visionaries. One
of its earliest practitioners appears to have been the German
mystic Gertrude the Great, who died right at the beginning
of the century, in 1302. Her *Revelations* are credited with
helping to establish medieval devotion to the Sacred Heart,
and it is late medieval stress on the human familiarity and

warmth of Christ's love which seems to encourage the idea of lengthy, intimate dialogues between Christ and the soul.

Later writers include Margery's favourite, St Bridget of Sweden (1303–73), and St Catherine of Siena (1347–80). Among male writers, there is Henry Suso (1295–1366), in his *Book of Eternal Wisdom*, and, as a minor example in England, the anonymous Monk of Farne.[8]

One of the problems with this kind of writing is that it is not clear to what extent we are dealing with a literary convention, by which a person's understanding of God would be expressed *as if* God himself were speaking, and to what extent the writers concerned are claiming these 'revelations' as real experiences. Rare are mystics such as Julian of Norwich, who distinguishes scrupulously throughout her work between the words of Christ (usually only a sentence or two) which actually form part of the visions she received, and what she herself understood by these words (expressed at far greater length), even though Christ tells her that her understanding of the visions forms an integral part of the whole revelation.[9]

If we are dealing primarily with a literary tradition, it is not difficult to see how it might have developed. It is interesting that many of Gertrude the Great's revelations took place in church, while she was attending the liturgy. This suggests that liturgical material might have had some influence on her, which does not seem unlikely, if we consider that one of the main building-blocks of the medieval liturgy, both in the Offices such as Matins and Vespers and in the Mass, was the Psalter. The psalms are, in effect, long intimate prayers – whether of praise, lament, outrage or peace – addressed to God, frequently by a single speaker. However, as part of the Bible, they could also be considered as part of God's own Word, addressed by him to mankind. Phrases from the psalms, as well as from other parts of the Old

Testament, were often combined in order to put words and sentiments into the mouth of Christ, over and beyond the ones we have in the Gospels. The material surrounding Holy Week and Easter, such as the 'Reproaches' ascribed to Christ in the liturgy of Good Friday, illustrates the process particularly well:

> O my people, what have I done to you, or in what have I offended you? Answer me. Because I led you out of the land of Egypt, you have prepared a cross for your Saviour ... What more should I have done for you, that I have not done? I, even I, planted you to be my fairest vineyard, and you have made yourself exceedingly bitter to me: for you have slaked my thirst with vinegar, and pierced with a lance your Saviour's side.[10]

Outside the liturgy, the tradition of using the psalms in prayer seems also to have led to the composition of lengthy 'colloquies', highly personal meditations composed as though addressed to God during the course of an intimate conversation. Ignatius of Loyola, inheriting this strand of medieval tradition, defines a colloquy as the conversation of a friend with a friend, or of a slave with his master, when he discusses what he has done wrong and asks for advice for the future.[11] Despite the conversational tone, only the human side of the interchange is recorded. The most formative examples of this kind of 'colloquy' were probably the two most popular works of St Augustine of Hippo, the *Soliloquies* and the *Confessions*. At the onset of the later Middle Ages, the *Meditations* of Anselm of Canterbury extended the tradition in the direction of even greater emotion and intimacy.[12]

Beyond these major works of devotional literature, which were written in Latin, popular piety in the late Middle Ages put many short lyrics into the mouth of Christ, composed in the vernacular, in which he woos the soul like a lover, or points to his sufferings on the cross and demands a response from the individual. In these short lyrics, the liturgical and devotional traditions can be seen to meet, and the impression of a dialogue can be created, although in a brief and delicate form.[13]

In the kind of late medieval work in which long conversations with God figure prominently, the 'colloquy' tradition seems to have been transposed on to God, so that he is now the one who speaks at length, while the meditator is often self-effacing.

As a purely literary device, the representation of long speeches in the mouth of Christ perhaps found its culmination in *The Imitation of Christ* of Thomas à Kempis (1380–1471), which he seems to have written around the time of his ordination to the priesthood in 1413.[14] The second half of this work (Books III and IV) takes the form of a dialogue between Christ and 'the disciple', with the dialogue being carefully introduced in a preliminary chapter, 'How Christ speaks inwardly to the soul'. Beginning with a sequence of quotations from Scripture, which establish the idea that God will speak within the soul of one who earnestly desires to listen to him, the chapter goes on, 'Your Beloved says: I am your Salvation, your Peace and your Life . . .'.[15] This phrase suggests the metaphorical putting of words into Christ's mouth, and the speeches of Christ follow on from there.

However, Margery herself seems to be writing more in the tradition of Bridget of Sweden and Catherine of Siena, both of whom received the discourses of Christ which they record during their times of ecstasy, that is, during extended periods of contemplative prayer of trance-like intensity. The discourses are therefore treated as given directly by God. In both cases, the works were dictated to priest-scribes at or soon after the time of the revelations themselves. Although

Bridget spoke in Swedish, her work was written down in Latin, and may therefore have been somewhat edited and interfered with by her translators.[16] In Catherine's case, however, her major work, *The Dialogue*, was dictated and recorded in her local Italian dialect. She asked her secretaries to be ready to take down anything she uttered while in ecstasy, and seems to have completed the work within a year. Not surprisingly, perhaps, the long, involved sentences of the original Italian seem to flow out in a torrent, and to be at times obscure.[17] Both these works circulated in English translations in Margery's lifetime, although she only mentions 'Bride's book' as being known to her. However, it is interesting that, as we saw in the Introduction, extracts from Margery were bound up by Henry Pepwell in 1521 in his *Miscellany*, in which the only other woman featured was Catherine of Siena, as though people recognised a likeness between the two.[18]

In the last chapter, we considered the visions, or visual 'contemplations', of Bridget of Sweden, in which she is led by the Virgin Mary through the scenes of Christ's life and passion. However, at the end of each visual section, there is a long meditation in which Christ himself speaks, commenting on the doctrinal import of the scenes that Bridget has just witnessed. In fact, the whole of the *Liber Celestis* opens with Christ himself addressing her:

> I am the maker of heaven and earth, one in Godhead with the Father and the Holy Spirit. I am he who spoke to the prophets and patriarchs, the one whom they all longed to see. To fulfil their desire, according to my promise, I have taken on manhood without any sin or concupiscence, entering the womb of a virgin as the sun shines through a block of crystal. Just as the sun, in shining, pierces the glass but does not hurt it, just so the virginity of my mother is not corrupted or defiled through the assumption of my manhood. . . .[19]

This opening is a good example of Christ's style of discourse throughout Bridget's book. More schoolmasterly than in Margery, he moves fairly briskly through a lot of sound doctrinal instruction, combining many scriptural allusions with standard medieval analogies and metaphors, such as the one used above for Christ's virgin birth. The discourses given after each visual section are also more tightly organised for the purposes of instruction, with much numbering of points – there are three types of evil people, God has two treasures in his house, he requires four things of us, and so on – which is somewhat reminiscent of Julian of Norwich's careful sub-dividing and ordering of her points, when she comments on her own visions. Margery may have got from Bridget, who calls herself simply 'the spouse', her habit of referring to herself in the third person as 'this creature', but otherwise we can see at once that Christ's discourse to her leaves a somewhat different impression, being, for the most part, more directly concerned with Margery's particular circumstances and calling.

If we turn to Catherine of Siena, we find a more flowing style, but again the main emphasis is on theological instruction. The generally more abstract and intellectual nature of Catherine's work, which is not built around a series of visual meditations as is Bridget's, is reflected in the sophistication with which the discourses are presented: in this case, it is not Christ, strictly speaking, who addresses Catherine, but 'Truth', who most of the time represents God the Father, but who also refers to Christ as 'my Truth'. Thus we can get passages such as the following:

> So you see, my Truth spoke the truth when he said, 'Those who love me will be one thing with me.' For when you follow his teaching you will be united with him in loving affection. And when you are united with him you are united with me, because

he and I are one. And once we are one, I will show myself to you. So my Truth spoke the truth when he said, 'I will show myself to you.' For when he showed himself he showed me, and when he showed me, he showed himself.[20]

Margery, then, is writing in a tradition in which other women visionaries had recorded long discourses of Christ, which they had received in prayer, by what they considered to be direct inspiration. However, there is one major difference between Margery and the two writers we have been considering: Bridget and Catherine both felt strongly that they were being given an understanding of theological matters specifically in order to share their insights; instruction is the core motivation of their work. With Margery, however, the discourses are written down only as part of her own spiritual odyssey, and chart the development of her understanding of her own vocation. This also perhaps contributed to E. I. Watkin's remark that her 'revelations are, almost to monotony, concerned with herself'.[21]

However, it is precisely this personal reference which makes them valuable in terms of our own understanding of Margery. For it is in these conversations with Christ that we see her own mysticism being articulated. Furthermore, although comparison with the steady high-flown sweep of the writings of Catherine and Bridget shows up Margery's gawky unevenness with particular clarity, it also reveals something more attractive: there is an endearing vulnerability and confusion about Margery, and a corresponding tenderness and detailed involvement on the part of Christ, which is lacking in the magisterial self-confidence of the other two. However much Catherine may give us a picture of an ardent soul, totally consumed by her desire for God and lost to any self-concern in her overwhelming concern for the Church as a whole, there is something more humanly believable about Margery, which, in the end, perhaps holds our attention more effectively.

Indeed, when we return to Margery's *Book* after considering other medieval works, as we have done above, much of the initial impression of sameness and lack of impact in the words of Christ disappears.

To begin with, even in the most intellectual discourse in Margery's book, the one on the Trinity, we notice in the words ascribed to Christ a more circumspect 'sometimes you think, daughter, that I . . .', rather than the straightforwardly didactic 'I am he who . . .' of Bridget and Catherine. Although the repeated 'you think . . . you also think . . .' might be interpreted as a mere verbal device, whereby Margery's understanding of the Trinity is simply recast as a speech in the mouth of Christ, it can also be taken to show a commendable diffidence on her part about her thought-processes. Christ thanks Margery for all her thoughts about him, but does not necessarily imply that they are to be taken as true, in any literal or absolute sense. This allows the discourse to include, without comment, a rather charming picture of the Trinity sitting on three cushions: the Father on one of gold, the Son on one of red velvet, and the Holy Spirit on one of white silk, with each cushion being given a symbolic interpretation.

Several critics have remarked on the awkward impression created by Margery's depictions of the actions and words of Christ, and this awkwardness arises, perhaps, from her sudden juxtapositions of rather abstract and high-flown terms with unexpectedly concrete language, as with the three cushions above. Further, the 'clerical voice' of the passages is occasionally punctuated with phrases of a homely vigour which can only have come from the mind of a medieval housewife: 'You stick to me as fast as the skin of a fish sticks to a man's hand when it is boiled' (ch. 37); 'You will be eaten and gnawed by the world as a rat gnaws the stock-fish' (ch. 5); 'Though he run every year to Jerusalem, I have no liking for him . . .' (ch. 34).

Thus, when we compare the speeches of Christ in Margery's book to the more sustained and polished discourses in other medieval works, the very unevenness of their tone and language lends them a certain distinctive colour, variety and impact.

In the next chapter, therefore, we will look at what we learn from these discourses of Margery's own distinctive spirituality, and relate this to other aspects of her experience.

Nine

MARGERY'S TEACHING

WE HAVE seen that the primary purpose of St Bridget of Sweden and St Catherine of Siena in their writings was to communicate spiritual instruction and theological insights, which were faithfully recorded and disseminated by their respective circles of priest-disciples. We noted that Margery's *Book* is not a theological treatise in the same way; that it is, rather, a far more personal record of her own conversion and individual spiritual journey. This does not mean, however, that her life did not have a public dimension, and that she did not have a message to communicate to others.

It is particularly necessary to consider this issue of her message, if any, in relation to the subject of her visions and conversations with Christ, for, as we have seen, the third major charge against her is that these visions and conversations, while comforting to herself, are not only at first sight unconvincing, but have nothing of value to offer anyone else.

In order to explore their possible value, we need to look at how the inner conversations throw light on what is happening outwardly in Margery's life. In fact, Christ's discourses help to draw together the various strands of the *Book*, and to bring out the significance of Margery's experience as a whole.

MARGERY'S ROLE AS A TEACHER

If we look in detail at the conversations, we see how a public dimension to Margery's life emerges very soon after the 'breakthrough' when Christ ravished her soul, after her first four years or so of intense ascetic life. The breakthrough is marked by the first of his long speeches (ch. 5). This initial communication is mostly taken up with specific instructions for the next stage of her life, such as not eating meat, and taking off her hair-shirt. As we saw in earlier chapters, she is also assured of forgiveness for her sins 'to the utterest point', which is important for the ensuing peacefulness or otherwise of her personality, and she is commanded to start praying with her mind. This first speech is obviously relevant only to Margery.

Already in the ensuing few months, however, even before John Kempe has agreed to her desire for celibacy, Christ starts telling Margery that those who hear her hear the voice of God, and that any sinner who repents and follows her counsels will receive grace (ch. 10). We see here the beginnings of her mission to go about among people rebuking them, telling improving stories, and urging them to amend their lives, a mission which, as we saw in the chapter on her trials for heresy, seems to have exasperated some of the Church authorities. Although this might look at first like Margery transposing incipient megalomania on to a supposed speech from God, what we see of this mission in action is striking, and not without its moving and tender side.

First of all, there is the sheer courage, and lack of any favour or flattery, with which she constantly rebukes the swearing and blasphemy which seem to have been in vogue among the various bishops' entourages at the time, along with modish clothes and behaviour. With characteristic directness and daring she begins at the top, telling the

Archbishop of Canterbury, when she goes to see him at Lambeth (ch. 16), that God will hold him responsible for his household, whose blasphemous language daily murders Christ all over again. He bears the rebuke meekly. When she visits the Bishop of Worcester, she scolds the clerics of his household for their extravagantly fashionable clothes, telling them they look more like the devil's men. They are first angry, then silenced (ch. 45). On trial before the Archbishop of York, she responds to the clerics who are reviling her by telling them that their oaths will send them to hell, for they are breaking the commands of God. Even in this situation, where she is the prisoner, some slink off, as if ashamed. Finally, she tells the Archbishop himself, when he says that he has heard she is a bad woman, that she has heard he is a bad man, and he will never get to heaven unless he amends his life while still on earth. Although outraged at first, the Archbishop manifestly develops a very real respect for Margery; this does not, however, dilute his strong desire to be rid of her.

While it is easy to see the irritation value of Margery's outspokenness, and to be astonished at her sheer lack of prudence, given that she is on trial for her life, there is a directness and impartiality here which somehow lend real authority to her rebukes. This, presumably, is what we see people responding to. Furthermore, in among her flat statements about the wrongness of certain kinds of conduct, there is now and then a mysteriously moving, almost poetic assertion: we can almost hear it find its mark in the other person's heart. Thus, before the Archbishop of York, she replies to his angry question about why she is weeping: 'Sir, you will wish one day that you had wept as bitterly as I.' And, as we saw when discussing her tears, she responds to a parish priest who had tried to quieten her cries before a crucifix: 'Sir, his death is as fresh to me now as if he had

died this same day, and so, I think, it should be to you and
to all Christian people.' (ch. 60).

As to the rest of her teaching ministry, we get two glimpses
of the sort of stories she tells. The first is at Canterbury (ch.
13), when she responds to the taunts of the monks with the
following tale. A man was ordered by his confessor to hire
men for one year to reprove him for his sins. One day he
found himself among powerful people who treated him with
contempt, which caused him to laugh. When they asked
him what he was laughing at, he explained that on that day
he was getting the rebukes, which he normally paid for, free,
and therefore he thanked them all. Right so, says Margery,
she thanks the monks of Canterbury. Needless to say, her
audience is enraged by this tale, and they run her out of
the monastery. If anything, this reaction confirms the tale's
spiritual appropriateness, and shows us something of the wry
humour and telling pungency of Margery's style of teaching.

The second example occurs when she is on trial before
the Archbishop of York at Cawood. She has already come
through her examination successfully, when one of the ques-
tioners tries to stir up more trouble for her by claiming that
she had told him the worst tale about priests he had ever
heard (ch. 52). At the Archbishop's command, she repeats
it. A priest went astray in a wood, and spent the night under
a beautiful pear-tree covered in blossom. An ugly bear came
and ate the blossoms, and then, turning round, expelled
them at the priest from his rear end. Disgusted, the priest
went on his way the next morning, and by chance met an
old man, who explained the meaning of what he had seen:
the pear-tree was the priest himself and the bear his blasphemous behaviour, for he performed all his services
without devotion, or any gratitude for the sacraments, and
spent the rest of his time in self-indulgence, idleness and
malicious gossip.

In this second case, Margery gets a better reception. The Archbishop commends the tale, and, more significantly, the same cleric who had provoked the telling of it comments: 'Sir, this tale smites me to the heart.' Here we see an instance of Margery's power to bring about conversion, but we also see her ongoing confrontational tactics. Rather than saying anything encouraging to the priest at this point, she turns on him with a personal rebuke, again quoting a mini-*exemplum*: a good cleric she knows says often that if someone dislikes his preaching, it is because that person is guilty of the sins he is describing; just so, says Margery, the priest at York is against her, because what she says applies to him. Abashed, he later asks her privately to forgive him and to pray for him.

Other incidents throughout the *Book* confirm Margery's power to 'smite to the heart'. Early on, there is the monk, referred to in connection with her prophetic feelings, who at first despises her, but who amends his whole life when she is able, without anyone telling her, to name in detail his secret sins (ch. 12). Then there is Thomas Marchale, who befriends her in Bristol, and is one of her two companions who get imprisoned in Leicester when she is arrested there. Of him, the *Book* says that he had been a 'reckless and misgoverned' man, but on meeting Margery he is overcome with repentance, being particularly moved by what she has to say of contrition and compunction (ch. 45). Even an enemy can be won over: one of the rather rough men who arrest Margery, in the hope of getting a hundred pounds for her from the Duke of Bedford, eventually says to her, addressing her with the courteous 'damsel': 'If ever you are a saint in heaven, pray for me.' (ch. 53).

A further example of the confidence that others have in the power of her prayers, not only to convert them in the first place but also to help them persevere in their new path, comes in her interview with the Bishop of Worcester (ch. 45). As previously mentioned, the Bishop knows Margery's family and summons her to meet him largely out of friendship. He hears her confession, and then confides in her that he has been told he will die within two years; he asks her to pray for him that he will die in charity, in the right spirit. We get the impression of a somewhat shaken and chastened man, who wants to see Margery, not so much to examine her, as for his own reassurance. There is a touching equality and intimacy about this particular encounter.

It is profoundly logical that Margery's teaching ministry should spring from her own experience of repentance and conversion, and that her ongoing contrition should be a strengthening example to others. In the chapter on tears, we saw how personal contrition quickly developed for Margery into contrition on behalf of the whole world, and into intercession on behalf of all sinners: 'I have ordained you to kneel before the Trinity to pray for all the world.' (ch. 7). In that chapter, which draws on many of the most important discourses of Christ to Margery, we concentrated on the inner dimension of that calling. However, it is apparent that Margery's spirituality has both an inner and an outer manifestation at each stage.

MARGERY AS A 'SIGN'

Above, the rather confrontational outer nature of Margery's teaching ministry was noted, and, inwardly, we see many early speeches of Christ dwelling on the opprobrium that she will have to bear, for she was often chided for her rebuking of sin. It is in this connection that she ponders on what death she would be willing to die for him, as mentioned before (ch. 14).

But more widely significant than provoking the anger of

her specific targets, is her role as 'a mirror' to other sinners, showing the kind of contrition they should have for their sins, and dramatically revealing God's power to turn around a whole life. We saw this power in the long discourse in which Christ compares his action to that of a range of natural cataclysms: destructive tempests, thunder and lightning, earthquakes (chs 77–8). What we can now consider is the fact that, outwardly as well, important moments in Margery's spiritual journey seem to have been marked by storms and tempests.

Physical phenomena cluster around Margery's time in Rome, during which she experiences her spiritual marriage to the Godhead, and the storms seem to be just one such phenomenon. The first seems to occur on St Bridget's Day, when Margery is visiting the saint's cell, and has had the touching experience of meeting Bridget's former maid-servant. Such storms of wind and rain occur that day that all outdoor work has to be abandoned, and Margery believes that the storms have been sent to 'hallow' the saint's feast-day (ch. 39). More personally, when she has returned to England, she asks God to confirm his injunction that she should wear white clothes by sending a storm of thunder and lightning, which he does on the following Friday (ch. 44). Again, when Margery's companions are imprisoned at Leicester, such tempests occur that the townspeople are convinced that this is a sign that Margery is a good woman, and that it is quite wrong to detain her two male companions. As soon as the two men have been hastily questioned and released, the weather turns fair again (ch. 47). There is also the incident when Margery puts out a major fire in Lynn by causing an unseasonal fall of snow, through her prayers for a storm or downpour of some kind (ch. 67).

What may at first seem to be rather pointless, if dramatic, phenomena take on meaning in the light of Christ's long

discourse to her about his work in men's souls being like the
effect of storms and tempests. Margery is obviously meant to
move about among her contemporaries with all the arresting
and disruptive power of a storm, dragging their minds away
from their usual concerns and forcing them to confront the
ultimate issues of sin and salvation. Early on, when she is
learning to intercede for sinners, Christ says to her: 'I send
them preaching and teaching, pestilence and battles,
hunger and famine, loss of their goods and great sickness,
and many other tribulations, and still they will not believe
my words or acknowledge my visitation.' (ch. 20).

Margery, it seems, is meant to be a sign of God's visitation.
She acts like a storm through her disruptive sobbing and bawl-
ing, which, as we saw before, God absolutely refuses to take
from her. When she asks that at least she might be released
from her shouting in church, she is told: 'Daughter, do not ask
for this; you shall not have your desire in this, even if my
mother and all the saints in heaven pray for you, for I shall
make you submissive to my will so that you will cry when I
wish, and where I wish, both quietly and out loud.' (ch. 77).

Right from the outset, the discourses emphasise that Margery's sobbing and tears are not within her control, even in
the early days when these are mainly motivated by contrition, as against the period after her journey to the Holy
Land, when the sufferings of Christ seem to become the
main focus: 'You cannot have tears or dalliance [with God]
except when God will send them to you.' (ch. 14).

EMPATHY FOR THE FLESH OF CHRIST

Even in these early days, however, we saw how her weeping
already passes rapidly into intense compassion for the sufferings of Christ. The connecting link here is found in the
doctrine that these sufferings were undertaken to win for-

giveness for human beings and to overcome their separation from God. This is expressed in powerful terms to Margery: 'I cannot forget you, how you are written into my hands and my feet . . . I swear to your mind, if it were possible for me to suffer pain again as I did before, I would sooner choose to suffer as much pain as I ever suffered for your soul alone, rather than that you should be parted from me without end.' (ch. 14).

As Margery's assurance of having received forgiveness for her sins grows, she seems to feel an ever stronger need simply to draw nearer to the humanity of Christ, and this leads her to go on pilgrimage to the Holy Land: she 'had a desire to see those places where he was born and where he suffered his Passion and where he died, with other holy places where he was in his life and also after his resurrection.' (ch. 15). As we saw in the chapter on Margery's journeys, her first 'crying', in the sense of shouting or screaming, occurred while in Jerusalem, at Mount Calvary. After Margery's return from the Holy Land, her most disruptive behaviour occurs at any mention of the passion of Christ, and whenever she receives communion.

As we saw in previous chapters, this sobbing and screaming on contemplating the sufferings of Christ was not unique to Margery. But there is another important manifestation of this compassion in Margery's daily life, which seems to be distinctive to her. This manifestation emerges chiefly after the spiritual marriage she experiences in Rome, which we will come back to.

This spiritual marriage seems to have transformed her seeing of human life, so that the most ordinary sights and sounds open like a window on to the one fundamental human life, that of Christ.

And sometimes, when she saw the crucifix, or if she saw that a man had a wound, or an animal – whichever it were – or if a man beat a child in front of her or struck a horse or other animal with a whip, if she saw or heard it, then she thought she saw our Lord being beaten or wounded, just as she saw it in the human being or in the animal; [this happened] as much in the fields as in the town, and alone by herself as much as among people. (ch. 28).

This important passage was one of the handful selected by Wynkyn de Worde for publication in 1501, which suggests that he too, or whoever originally selected the passages, was struck by its distinctiveness.

Thereafter, there are similar passages throughout the *Book*:

She was so deeply attached to the manhood of Christ, that when she saw women in Rome carrying children in their arms, if she was able to find out that there were any boys among them, she would cry out, roar and weep as though she had seen Christ himself when he was a child. And if she could have had what she wanted, she would often have taken the children from their mothers' arms and kissed them in Christ's stead. And if she saw a good-looking man, she had great difficulty in looking at him, in case she might have seen the one who was both God and man. And therefore, when she met a good-looking man, she often cried out many times and wept and sobbed most bitterly over the manhood of Christ as she went through the streets of Rome, so that those who saw her wondered at her very much, because they did not know the cause of her weeping. (ch. 35).

Similarly, when she visits Leicester Abbey after her release from trial, she sees the Abbot of Leicester approaching with his monks, and sees in him Christ approaching with his apostles; she is so overcome that she has to lean against a pillar, until her cries have passed (ch. 49). Likewise, in all churchings of women, held forty days after childbirth, she sees the purification of Mary and the presentation of Christ in the Temple, when the aged Simeon took the infant Christ in his arms (ch. 82).

Most strikingly of all, perhaps, she sees in any sick man the wounded Christ, particularly in lepers; when she meets them in the street, she is overcome with sorrow and frustration that she cannot kiss them. Strictly barred by her confessor, for reasons of propriety, from kissing any men, she has to content herself with seeking out some female lepers and kissing them – an act of real tenderness and courage, considering the fear and disgust that their disease inspired (ch. 74).

That the natural world should mediate to people an intense awareness of the presence of God is nothing new; but that the ordinary bustle of human life should do so is distinctive to Margery. Nearly all the medieval mystics, including Margery's chief model, Bridget of Sweden, took it as axiomatic that a degree of separation from the hurly-burly of the world was necessary to the development of their mystical communion with God. Bridget, for example, wished eventually to become a nun and founded her own enclosed, contemplative order. Not so Margery: she extracts from the medieval spiritual tradition the need to spend many hours in prayer, but she does this mainly in her local church; she also believes in the centrality of celibacy, but, having made her vow of chastity, does not envision living anywhere but with her family. Although gossip eventually forces her to live apart from her husband until the last few years of his life, she never expresses the slightest wish to withdraw from the normal urban environment in which she has always spent her life. For Margery, the equivalent of the cloister – the physical environment which fosters and supports her prayer-life – is the local town, and many of her experiences of intense communion with Christ come to her as she walks

about the streets, observing the perfectly ordinary occur-
rences of human life.

If Margery has a contribution of her own to make to
the medieval mystical tradition, I suggest it is here, in this
'consecration', as it were, of the noise and movement of
ordinary life. However, it is not just the events of human
life, such as the routine churching of women after childbirth, which she focuses on. As we saw in the quotations
above, it is particularly human flesh, in its vulnerability,
which calls forth her perception of Christ in the human
being before her eyes. For Margery, it is the flesh that
becomes the central meeting-point between man and God,
the place where their relationship is forged. As Christ says
to her: 'You have so great compassion for my flesh that I
must needs have compassion on your flesh.' (ch. 77).
Margery, surely, takes what we might call incarnational mysticism to its furthest point.

Mystical Spouse and Mother

This compassion becomes the focus in Margery's thinking
for all the ways she can express her relationship to Christ.
In an early discourse, he says to her:

> When you seek to please me, then you are truly a daughter;
> when you weep and mourn for my pain and for my Passion,
> then you are truly a mother who feels compassion for her child;
> when you weep for other men's sins and for adversities, then
> you are truly a sister; and, when you lament because you are
> separated for so long from the bliss of heaven, then you are truly
> a spouse and a wife, for it belongs to the nature of a wife to be
> together with her husband, and to have no true joy until she
> comes into his presence. (ch. 14).

The imagery of the spouse is central to medieval tradition,

being based ultimately on Scripture: in the Old Testament, the Song of Songs was interpreted as a mystical treatise describing the relationship of the soul to God in terms of the relationship between bride and bridegroom; in the New Testament, there are the parables of the wise and foolish virgins and of the wedding guest without a garment, and in the Book of Revelation everyone participates in the wedding banquet of the Lamb.

Furthermore, the experience of a 'spiritual marriage' is a phenomenon recorded by several other mystics in the late medieval period.[1] In nearly every case, the 'marriage' takes place during a vision, in which the mystic is espoused to Christ in a ritual reflecting the marriage formulas in use at the time. There is usually a sense of pomp and celebration about this espousal, with many heavenly witnesses being present, chief among them the Virgin Mary. St Catherine of Siena is perhaps the most notable example, whose account may have had a formative influence on later saints reporting the same phenomenon. In Catherine's case, the Virgin Mary took her by the hand, and in the presence of St John the Evangelist, St Paul, St Dominic, and King David playing his harp, presented her to Christ, who gave her a ring with the words: 'I marry you to me in faith, to me, your Creator and Saviour. Keep this faith unspotted until you come to me in heaven and celebrate the marriage that has no end.' He then bids her to be courageous in everything that he will ask her to do.[2]

In Margery's case, the formula of marriage is obviously borrowed from the wedding rite current in England at the time: 'I take you, Margery, for my wedded wife, for fairer, for fouler, for richer, for poorer, as long as you are gentle and submissive in doing what I command you.' (ch. 35). There is an engaging familiarity about this formula, which at the same time creates a somewhat pedestrian effect, especially when compared to the scriptural and theological awareness reflected in the wording of St Catherine's account. Surprisingly, however, Margery's more down-to-earth language is situated in a potentially more rarefied and less concrete marriage ceremony. In her case, it is not Mary who takes her by the hand to espouse her to Christ, but Christ who stands by as she is wed to the Father. In one of the few passages in Margery's book which conveys a real sense of religious awe, she is dumbfounded with fear at the approach of the Father when he says to her, 'Daughter, I will have you wedded to my Godhead, for I shall show you my private secrets and my counsels, for you are to live with me without end.' Margery, who previously has so blithely assured us of her chatty relations with each of the three Persons of the Trinity (ch. 17), now tells us: 'Then the creature kept silence in her soul and gave this no answer, for she was sorely afraid of the Godhead, and she knew nothing of the dalliance of the Godhead, for all her love and all her affection were set on the manhood of Christ . . .'. Nonetheless, Christ having asked her for her consent, the Father takes her by the hand and, in the presence of a great multitude of angels and saints, utters the words of espousal quoted above (ch. 35).

That this 'mystical marriage' represented an important step forward in Margery's spiritual journey is suggested by the new developments that follow from it. After this, she experiences a number of physical phenomena, lasting for many years: apart from the storms mentioned above, she became aware of sweet smells, heavenly melodies, and many white specks of light flying about her, which she takes as signs that angels are around her to protect her. She also experienced, for about sixteen years, a burning heat in her breast which closely resembles the 'fire of love' described by Richard Rolle in his most famous work, the *Incendium*

Amoris. There are trials as well: she feels the urge to give away all her money, and she seems to have lived on the brink of destitution for the rest of her life; she is also wracked by ill-health for years, to the extent that she is twice given the last rites, as we saw in the chronology of her life. Most importantly, however, there is the opening of her spiritual vision, as described above, whereby she henceforth sees Christ in and through every human situation she encounters.

In spite of this marriage, with its spousal imagery, for Margery the mother-child relationship is the one she most relates to emotionally, with herself in the role of mother, and Christ as the child whom she cares for and who, in return, cares for her. Christ repeatedly promises her that he will be an obedient son to her, and commends her for being a true mother to him: 'Daughter, there was never child so subservient to his father as I shall be to you, to help and protect you' (ch. 14); 'You are to me a real mother and to all the world because of the great charity that is in you' (ch. 36). We also saw, in connection with her visions, how Margery tends the infant Christ in her imagination, and how he thanks her for this.

In the great discourse on the Trinity near the end of her book, Christ further says to her: 'You call my mother to come into your soul, and take me in her arms, and lay me to her breast and give me suck.' (ch. 86). This striking image helps us understand the place of Margery's deep devotion to the Virgin Mary within her overall spirituality: she responds to her not so much as to a sinless virgin who was the most steadfast follower of Christ on earth, but as to the mother of his physical body. In growing close to Mary, Margery hopes to grow more deeply into the experience of being a mother to Christ.

It is Margery's compassion for the flesh of Christ which

seems to make her respond so readily to the role of mother; this compassion she feels to be in essence not wifely, but maternal. Once again, Margery seems here to be making a distinctive contribution to medieval spirituality, using the sheer physicality of the experience of motherhood, with its concern for the physical well-being of the child, as a way of entry into a relationship with God. In a religious culture where monastic celibacy, and therefore physical childlessness, was taken as the spiritual ideal, Margery is breaking new ground here, taking the very experience and preoccupation which might seem to *despiritualise* her as the central element in her own mysticism.

The mother-child imagery is so central to Margery's spiritual life that it invades even the scene of her mystical marriage to the Godhead. The formula of espousal, which we looked at above, continues immediately in perhaps surprising language:

> I take you, Margery, for my wedded wife, for fairer, for fouler, for richer, for poorer, as long as you are gentle and submissive in doing what I command you. For, daughter, there was never child so obedient to its mother as I shall be to you, both in prosperity and in woe, to help you and comfort you. (ch. 35).

After listing some of the physical phenomena which ensue from the marriage, there follows a long discourse which contains the most striking passage of erotic language in Margery. Yet even here the mother-son relationship intrudes:

> Therefore I must needs be intimate with you, and lie in your bed with you. Daughter, you desire greatly to see me, and you may boldly, when you are in your bed, take me to you as your wedded husband, as your darling, and as your sweet son, for I want to be loved as a son should be loved by the mother, and I want you to love me, daughter, as a good wife ought to love her husband. Therefore you may boldly take me in the arms of

your soul and kiss my mouth, my head, and my feet as sweetly as you wish.' (ch. 36).

This passage is striking in the sense that, although the imagery of Christ as lover was a commonplace of medieval spirituality, with the sexual relationship taken as a perfectly acceptable metaphor for the soul's union with God, Margery's language veers rather more than usual from the metaphorical into the literal.[3]

UNION WITH THE GODHEAD

This problem of awkward language, combined with Margery's intense focus on the flesh of Christ, might lead us to imagine that she would have very earth-bound and literal ways of expressing the union with the Godhead that is promised her in the mystical marriage, and which is the goal of her whole journey. However, her thinking here shows itself to be surprisingly sophisticated.

If we begin with what she has to say about the experience of *lacking* this union, we might expect to find in Margery sensational visions of the torments of hell, a favourite topic in the religious treatises of the period. Instead, hell is quite simply separation from the face of God: she wishes that no man may 'be parted endlessly from your glorious face' (ch. 57). Likewise, her weeping for sinners includes the souls in purgatory, for she wishes they were out of their pain, purely in order that they might have the joy of praising God without end. Conversely, heaven is the presence of God: 'Wheresoever God is, heaven is, and God is in your soul' (ch. 14). Her own reward in heaven will be to know clearly how much God loved her on earth, and to 'see without end every good day that I ever gave you on earth of contemplation, of devotion, and of all the great charity that I have given you for the benefit of your fellow-Christians.' (ch. 64).

There is, then, underlying Margery's overwhelming sense of contrition for herself and all sinners, an intense joy in simply beholding the presence of God. This is the joy of heaven which set her weeping in the first place at her conversion, when she exclaimed: 'Alas that ever I sinned! It is full merry in heaven.' (ch. 3).

When she is unable to weep, she tastes the separation from God that she fears for others:

> I am a hid God in your soul, and I withdraw sometimes your tears and your devotion . . . so that you should truly know what pain it is to forego my presence, and how sweet it is to feel me, and that you should apply yourself all the more to seeking me again; and also, daughter, so that you should know what pain other men have, who want to feel me and cannot. For there is many a man on earth, who, if he had but one day in his whole lifetime of the kind that you have many of, he would always love me the better, and thank me for that one day. (ch. 84).

In heaven, then, Margery will relive 'every day of contemplation' that she had on earth. This implies that Margery is already experiencing union with God, at least in some degree, in her inner contemplations. And, despite all the outward controversy, noisiness and disruptiveness that this chapter has examined, it is actually this contemplation which occupies her for the major part of each and every day of her life. It is desire for growth in contemplation which is the driving-force behind every outer event in her life: this is what drives her to go on pilgrimage; this is what sends her about the country to seek counsel from other contemplatives, even if, on the way, she gets arrested and tried for heresy. This is what causes her to wish to share in the poverty of Christ. Under all the outer drama, there is a profoundly still core.

Conclusion

WAS MARGERY A MYSTIC?

NOW THAT we have completed our survey of the main elements of Margery's life, we can address the issue of whether she was in any sense a genuine mystic, or whether the various charges levelled against her, which we have been discussing, do in the end disqualify her. Here we have to take into account our own position in history in relation to hers.

Margery fulfils the main criteria that a medieval audience looked for in a mystic. Chief among these were orthodoxy of doctrine, and observance of the commandments and virtues incumbent upon all Christians. As we saw, Margery came triumphantly out of all her trials for heresy, and no one charged her with any outright misconduct; she did not, for example, use her claims as a mystic to obtain large amounts of money, or go about spreading slander about other people. Secondly, the medieval authorities would have looked for signs of conversion in her whole life-style, and would have expected to find a sustained practice of asceticism, penance and long periods of prayer. These Margery demonstrated throughout her life.

Next, someone called to a life of devotion clearly beyond the ordinary would have been expected to observe, as nearly as possible in their circumstances, the three monastic principles of chastity, poverty and obedience. Here, Margery's costly vow of celibacy within marriage would have been seen as a strong sign of her authenticity, and it is probably this, more than any other aspect of her life, which accounts for the generally respectful and sympathetic audience she gains from all the high-ranking bishops and clerics with whom she has dealings. In addition, she ends up living a life of poverty, and throughout her *Book* we find her being deeply obedient to her confessors. The one apparent exception shows how much this obedience meant to her: she feels the Holy Spirit urging her to go to Germany with her daughter-in-law, when she is already on the coast out of reach of her confessor, and cannot consult him, leading to great inner turmoil (Book II, ch. 2). She resolves the turmoil by consulting a local priest, who urges her to follow her inner promptings. Without this instinctive turning to authority for advice, we might be tempted to think that Margery, in sight of a ship and the sea, has simply had an attack of wanderlust and is, for convenience, calling this the Holy Spirit. Even if there is an element of this, Margery's habit of self-doubt and obedience manifests itself the more strongly.

Further, from her deep repentance of sin and ongoing contrition comes, as we saw, the ability to bring about conversion of heart in others. This beneficent effect on the souls of others would have been seen as an important means of judging the healthiness or otherwise of the various supernatural phenomena that Margery reports: her visions, conversations with Christ, the lights she sees, sounds she hears, and heat she feels in her breast. As we saw, Margery and those around her are quite aware that these manifestations need not come from God, but could come from an evil source; one of Margery's salient characteristics is her constant referring of her thoughts and feelings to her confessors to check 'if there were any deceit in them'.

Nonetheless, one of the ways in which the medieval period

differed from the succeeding period of the Renaissance was in the place it accorded such supernatural phenomena: so long as they seemed to come from God and not from the devil, they were seen as a positive sign that supernatural grace was being received, rather than as an insignificant and rather tiresome side-effect, as implied in the writings of St Teresa of Avila and St John of the Cross.[1] Richard Rolle, who wrote enthusiastically of the experience of feeling heat and hearing heavenly melody, is a typical medieval in this sense, but even within his own century people were alarmed at the naivety of reading too much significance into such physical experiences. Even in the Renaissance, however, Teresa and John of the Cross were probably listened to because their own supernatural experiences, such as levitation, conferred a certain spiritual authority upon them in the eyes of their readers.

When it comes to some of the content of the visions and conversations, we have seen how most of what Margery reports can be situated within existing medieval traditions of devotion. The problem has been to decide quite on what level we should understand her statements of seeing, hearing and experiencing. The spiritual marriage, which we looked at in the last chapter, is a good example of the problem. Not only are we looking back at a medieval account of spiritual experiences from the rather sceptical and secular culture of the twentieth century, but we are also looking back through the filter of Renaissance teaching on the spiritual life, which, because it was also the period of the Reformation and the Counter-Reformation, has had a particularly formative influence on the religious thought of the following centuries.

The Renaissance was a great period of systematising of the spiritual life, sorting its various manifestations into evidence for clearly defined stages of progress on a narrowly

defined mystical path; this sorting and clarification was felt
to be crucial in a period deeply preoccupied by the fear of
religious error and delusion. In Teresa of Avila's *Interior
Castle*, the spiritual marriage is seen as a sign of the seventh
and highest mansion.[2] Are we, then, to read Margery as
claiming to have reached the very pinnacle of the mystical
life? It seems probable that back in the more fluid systems
of the Middle Ages, she would not have seen herself as
making a claim to a clearly defined position on a clearly
mapped-out spiritual path. Rather, the spiritual marriage
can perhaps be seen as one of the powerful symbols that
summon her onwards in her spiritual journey. We must not
over-hastily disqualify her because, in the terms of a later
age, she seems to be claiming more than she probably is.

On the other hand, a detailed comparison of the elements
of Margery's inner life, as recorded in her *Book*, with the
various 'mansions' described by Teresa, would probably
show Margery to have all the signs of being advanced in
contemplative prayer. The problem is that she is not setting
out her account as an orderly progression through various
stages. As we saw in the Introduction, she groups her
material instead by subject matter, dealing with visits to
spiritual directors in one sequence of chapters, prophetic
gifts in another, ministry to others in a third, and so on.

Furthermore, there is the problem of uneven language,
which lends her account an awkward effect, so that we are
not sure whether she herself understands something literally
or metaphorically. Interestingly, she herself acknowledges
this difficulty: 'Sometimes what she understood physically
was to be understood spiritually' (ch. 89). Although she
seems to be referring here specifically to her prophetic gifts,
could not this be a general problem for her with everything
that was revealed to her?

She also has the problem, not shared by Catherine or

Bridget or most other medieval women mystics, that her priest-scribe seems himself to have been one of the very ordinary lower clergy, without great theological sophistication or knowledge. In most other cases, the female mystic is helped to express herself by highly trained clerics, who probably instinctively serve to keep the focus on what is of central importance. Margery's scribe, however, on the few occasions when he interrupts the text in his own voice, shows a tendency to dwell on the sensational outer features of Margery's life. Thus the two chapters we have on her prophetic gifts seem to have been inserted largely at his instigation (chs 23–4). He tells us, without self-censure, that he pressed her to use her prophetic gifts, although she was extremely reluctant to do so, in view of the enormous mental stress and turmoil that this side of her life caused her. Some of the awkward, slightly confused impression given by her work could therefore be put down to pressure from her priest-scribe and her immediate audience.

There remains the fact that all those charged with passing authoritative judgement on her throughout her life – from the Papal Legate at Constanza and the Archbishops of Canterbury and York, down through the Bishops of Lincoln and Worcester and the Abbot of Leicester, to the priests and friars who were her usual confessors – accepted her as genuine.

This is a testament to the different values of the medieval period compared to those of our own day, the latter so suspicious of spiritual 'phenomena' and so quick to dismiss as unbalanced anyone who steps out of the standard secular patterns of behaviour. One wonders how a woman who was so spectacularly disruptive in church, distinctive in dress, and generally embarrassing in her conduct, would be received nowadays by the authorities of any Christian denomination. Although she would perhaps be treated compassionately in some quarters, would she be listened to with any real respect? The fact that she had lived through one clearly psychotic episode would probably disqualify her permanently as a genuine mystic in modern eyes. With our greater scientific knowledge of mental states, we tend to assume that where we can distinguish between healthy and unhealthy states of mind, the religiously obsessed Middle Ages could not. Consequently, we suspect that Margery was viewed as a mystic precisely *because* she was unbalanced; that her mysticism *consisted in* the symptoms of her mental illness. But, as we have seen, *The Book of Margery Kempe* makes a sharp distinction between her post-partum psychosis and the rest of her experiences.

However, there remains the problem of Margery's difficult personality. Would not a drawing closer to God make her less bombastic, less self-preoccupied, calmer, more stable in her life? When we look at the proportions of Margery's narrative, we do see this happening. Out of a spiritual journey covering twenty years from the time of her conversion, the last fifteen years – three-quarters of the time – are spent quietly in Lynn, nursing her husband, among others, praying at people's deathbeds, and generally simply getting on with her many hours of prayer. Further, one aspect of Margery's character, as opposed to the superficial aspects of her personality, which emerges strongly from the *Book* is her enormous talent for friendship. As we saw in the chapter on her journeys, for her foreign travel is a tale of people encountered, not of places visited. With her spiritual friends and advisers, she seems to have been able to form deep, peaceable and lasting relationships.

As to the self-preoccupation, here we come to the crux. This is what chiefly causes a recoil in modern readers, for we seem to expect self-effacement in a religious work. But what at first sight looks like bombast in Margery, on second reading can look more like deep insecurity. Let us, for example, go back to her first 'contemplation', when she serves the Virgin Mary and the Christ-child. We can observe the repeated praise for Margery from Mary and Elizabeth, or we can notice the touching lack of confidence in Margery's pleas for acceptance: she kneels to Mary and says she is not worthy to serve her; she begs Elizabeth to ask Mary on her behalf if she can go on serving her.

Whatever the unconfessed sin that led to Margery's bout of insanity when she was a young woman of twenty, it could be that it left a deep doubt about her acceptability in her mind. Although her madness never recurred, and although she seems truly to have felt herself forgiven, we saw that there remained a kind of pressure on Margery's mind, implied in Christ's words to her: 'I have chastised you myself as I wished by many great dreads and torments that you have had with evil spirits, both sleeping and waking, for many years . . .' (ch. 22). What we see in Margery, I suggest, is a personality under pressure, which gives her the curious mixture of self-doubt and courage, inter-personal clumsiness and lasting friendships, which we have commented on. While she was fully restored to sanity, it is as though a scar was left in her mind in some way. While this scarred personality may be at first unattractive, it is interesting that all the scholars who have produced serious studies of her, such as Hope Allen, Katherine Cholmeley, Clarissa Atkinson and others, eventually find themselves won over by her bemusing but touching mixture of self-doubt and un-self-critical truthfulness.

Finally, the last chapter argued that Margery definitely has something to say that is of value to others. Her mysticism lies in seeing Christ through the medium of the human beings she encounters as she goes about her normal business in the streets, and the reality of the presence she encounters is so overwhelming that she sobs, roars and screams. Surely, her chief function for her contemporaries was as a reminder, so vocal and vivid it could not be ignored, of the over-whelming reality of the God she perceived.

NOTES

INTRODUCTION

1. *The Times*, 27 December 1934, p. 15.
2. S. B. Meech and H. E. Allen, eds, *The Book of Margery Kempe*, Early English Text Society o.s. 212 (Oxford, 1940; reprinted 1961), xxxii.
3. The most famous example is perhaps the 'Amherst' manuscript, now British Library MS. Additional 37790. Originally in the possession of a Carthusian monk of Sheen, James Grenehalgh, it was bought by Lord Amherst in the seventeenth century. It contains many works of Richard Rolle, the crucial 'Short Text' of Julian of Norwich, and several unique texts of other devotional works.
4. 'Liber Montis Gracie. This boke is of Mountegrace' is written on the verso of the binding-leaf, just before the first page of the text. The manuscript has annotations almost certainly made by monks of Mount Grace.
5. Clarissa Atkinson, 'In Memoriam: Hope Emily Allen (1883–1969)', *14th Century English Mystics Newsletter* [now *Mystics Quarterly*], IX (1983), 210–15; also Meech and Allen, lxi.
6. British Library MS. Additional 61823.
7. For the text of Wynkyn de Worde's extracts, see Meech and Allen, *The Book*, Appendix II, 353–7. The pamphlet itself is in Cambridge University Library, Sel. 5, 27. This is the only

known copy: cf. C. E. Gordon Duff, *Hand-Lists of English Printers, 1501–1556* (London, 1913) i, 24.

8. Henry Pepwell's miscellany is in the British Library, C. 37. A second copy is in Trinity College, Cambridge. These appear to be the only two surviving copies.

9. Edmund G. Gardner, *The Cell of Self-Knowledge* (London and New York, 1910).

10. Ibid., p. 51. Cf. Meech and Allen, 30 (in ch. 14) and 353.

11. Gardner, pp. xx–xxi.

12. David Knowles, *The English Mystics* (London, 1927), ch. 6, 128–9.

13. Col. William Butler-Bowdon, *The Book of Margery Kempe, 1436* (London, 1936).

14. This is the edition given in note 2.

15. David Knowles, *The English Mystical Tradition* (London, 2nd ed., 1964), 148.

16. See, for example, Roy Porter, *A Social History of Madness: Stories of the Insane* (London, 1987), ch. 6: 'Mad Women', 103–112. This is one of the most compassionate and perceptive studies of Margery.

17. See, for example, Sheila Delany, 'Sexual Economics, Chaucer's Wife of Bath and the *Book of Margery Kempe*', *Minnesota Review*, n.s. 5, 104–13; Antony Goodman, 'The Piety of John Brunham's Daughter of Lynn', in *Medieval Women*, ed. Derek Baker (Oxford, 1978), 347–59; Karma Lochrie, '*The Book of Margery Kempe*: The Marginal Woman's Quest for Literary Authority', *Journal of Medieval and Renaissance Studies*, 16 (1986), 33–55.

CHAPTER ONE

1. See Hope Allen, *The Times*, 27 December 1934, p. 15; Barry Windeatt, trans., *The Book of Margery Kempe*, Penguin Classics (Harmondsworth, 1985), 9.

2. Meech and Allen, Appendix III, sections 1–3, 358–68. This Appendix (358–75) gives all the known external references to Margery Kempe; her father John Brunham, who was several

times Mayor of Lynn; her husband John Kempe; his father, also called John Kempe; and her brother-in-law Simon Kempe. Later sections refer to various clerics with whom she was in contact.

3. The evidence is discussed in Meech and Allen, 269, and Windeatt, 305.

4. See, for example, Margaret Archer, ed., *The Register of Bishop Philip Repingdon*, vol. 1, Lincoln Record Society 57 (Hereford, 1963), l, li n. Margery went to the Bishop of Lincoln to ratify her vow of celibacy, rather than to the Bishop of her own diocese, Norwich, probably because the see was vacant between 28 April 1413 (when Bishop Alexander died) and 11 September 1413 (when the new Bishop, Richard Courtenay, was consecrated). The latter was primarily a diplomat and was constantly away from Norwich on missions for the king, cf. *Victoria County History of Norfolk*, ed. William Page (London, 1906), vol. 2, 246–7.

5. John C. Hirsch, 'Author and Scribe in the *Book of Margery Kempe*', *Medium Aevum*, 44 (1975), 145–50.

6. For Rolle's Middle English text, see Hope Emily Allen, ed., *English Writings of Richard Rolle* (Oxford, 1931; reprinted 1963), 17–36; for a modern English version, see Rosamund Allen, ed. and trans., *Richard Rolle: The English Writings*, Classics of Western Spirituality (London and Mahwah, New Jersey, 1989), 90–124.

7. Butler-Bowdon, Appendix, 345–74.

8. Meech and Allen, xxxiii, 254.

CHAPTER TWO

1. We obtain this date by working backwards from the most firmly ascertained date in Margery's life, her vow of celibacy in 1413.

2. Margery's chronology is difficult to follow here. She says this period lasts 'three or four years', but then refers to an initial two years of grace followed by three years of temptation, which would give a total of five years. Later again, she says the period of temptation lasted one year.

3. See, for example, Edward I. Watkin, *Poets and Mystics* (London and New York, 1953), ch. 6: 'In defense of Margery Kempe', 120.

4. See Meech and Allen, 315, note on 125/$_{34-37}$.

5. Meech and Allen, 269; Windeatt, 305.

6. For the Lollards, see below, Chapter 6.

7. A brief account of Marie d'Oignies is given in Windeatt, 19–20; the standard account is the Latin text *Vita Mariae Oigniacensis* by Jacques de Vitry, in *Acta Sanctorum*, 25 (Brussels, 1867), 542–72; this account is also available in French: *Vie de Marie d'Oignies par Jacques de Vitry*, tr. André Wankenne, Société des Etudes Classiques (Namur, 1989).

CHAPTER THREE

1. E. Colledge, *Pre-Reformation English Spirituality* (New York, 1966), 222.

2. Roy Porter, *A Social History of Madness*, ch. 6: 'Mad Women', 103–112.

3. Raymond of Capua, *The Life of St Catherine of Siena*, trans. George Lamb (London, 1960), 92–3. The more restrained language here is probably due to Raymond's drawing a discreet veil over this episode in the life of his revered friend, and casting it in more conventionally pious terms. Margery's untutored frankness of style is perhaps one of the positive results of the fact that neither she nor her scribe were highly trained writers – unlike Raymond, who ended up as Master-General of the Dominican Order.

4. For examples of Richard Rolle's screaming see *The Fire of Love*, trans. Clifton Wolters, Penguin Classics (London, 1972), Chapter 26, p. 123; Chapter 33, p. 146; for a description of physical phenomena, Chapter 15, p. 93; for his aggressive tone towards his detractors, Chapter 13, pp. 82–4 and Chapter 15, p. 92. For a contemporary discussion of Rolle's controversial stress on physical phenomena see 'The Defence Against the Detractors of Richard by Thomas Basset, hermit', in H. E. Allen,

Writings Ascribed to Richard Rolle and Materials for his Biography (New York and Oxford, 1927), pp. 527–37.

5. Stephen Medcalf, ed., *The Later Middle Ages* (London, 1981), 114–15.

6. Windeatt, 300–301.

7. Trudy Drucker, 'The Malaise of Margery Kempe', *New York State Journal of Medicine*, 72 (1972), 2911–17.

8. The origins of this idea can be traced to the writings of St Ambrose of Milan (339–97), particularly to his two short treatises *Concerning Virgins* and *Concerning Widows*, which can be found in English in: Ambrose, *Select Works and Letters*, trans. H. de Romestin, Library of the Nicene and Post-Nicene Fathers, 2nd series, vol. 10 (Oxford and New York, 1896), 363–87 and 391–407. These writings lie behind the Middle English text *Heili Meidhad*, ed. Bella Millett, Early English Text Society o.s. 284 (London, 1982). This text was aimed primarily at nuns, but a secular text with a wider audience, which also clearly sets forth the threefold hierarchy of virgins, widows and spouses, is William Langland's *Piers Plowman*, Passus 16: 67–72, ed. A. V. C. Schmidt, Everyman (London, 1978), 200. There are several modern translations, e.g. A. V. C. Schmidt, *Piers Plowman: A New Translation*, World's Classics (Oxford, 1992), 190.

9. Medcalf, 116–17.

CHAPTER FOUR

1. *The Principle Works of St Jerome*, trans. W. H. Fremantle, Library of the Nicene and Post-Nicene Fathers, 2nd series, vol. 6 (Oxford and New York, 1893), Letter CXXII, 225–9.

2. See the article 'Larmes', *Dictionnaire de Spiritualité*, vol. 9 (Paris, 1976), 287–303.

3. See Lenten material in *Sarum Missal*, ed. J. Wickham Legg (Oxford, 1916), 48–115.

4. Wickham Legg, *Sarum Missal*, 402.

5. John Climacus, *The Ladder of Divine Ascent*, trans. Colm Luib-

heid and Norman Russell, Classics of Western Spirituality (New York and Toronto, 1982), 136–45, at 137.

6. Climacus, *The Ladder*, 68. For a discussion of the translation by the Franciscan Angelus Clarenus (thirteenth or early fourteenth century), see J. Gribomont, 'La *Scala Paradisi*, Jean de Raithou et Ange Clareno', *Studia Monastica* 2 (1960), 345–58.

7. Walter Hilton, *The Ladder of Perfection*, trans. Leo Sherley-Price, Penguin Classics (London, 1957), 37–40.

8. Richard Rolle, *The Fire of Love*, trans. Clifton Wolters, Penguin Classics (London, 1972). Rolle's references to tears and shouts tend to be rather fleeting: e.g. ch. 26, p. 123; ch. 33, p. 146.

9. *Vie de Marie d'Oignies par Jacques de Vitry*, tr. André Wankenne, Société des Etudes Classiques (Namur, 1989): vow of celibacy, 12; the incident repeated by Margery's scribe, of the priest who had criticised her being himself overcome by uncontrollable weeping, 14.

10. For the Latin text of her life, see Paul Doncoeur, *Le Livre de la Bienheureuse Angèle de Foligno* (Toulouse, 1925); also Paul Lachance, *The Spiritual Journey of Angela of Foligno* (London, 1985).

11. 'Et quia inceperam viam praedictam et rogaveram Deum quod morentur, magnam consolationem inde habui scilicet de morte eorum.' (Doncoeur, *Angèle de Foligno*, 10.)

12. 'Strixerat multum . . . venerant illuc ad videndum illam stridentem vel vociferantem.' (Doncoeur, *Angèle de Foligno*, 21). On a second visit to Assisi some time later, she has a similar experience (p. 28).

13. The sources are listed in Doncoeur, xii–xix.

14. Katherine Cholmeley, *Margery Kempe: Genius and Mystic* (London, New York, Toronto, 1947), 96–9; Edward I. Watkin, *Poets and Mystics* (London and New York, 1953), ch. 6: 'In defense of Margery Kempe', 104–35; Clarissa Atkinson, *Mystic and Pilgrim: The Book and the World of Margery Kempe* (Ithaca and London, 1983), ch. 5, 129–90.

CHAPTER FIVE

1. Meech and Allen, 364.
2. Meech and Allen, 359–62.
3. 'When they were sick': *Geoffrey Chaucer, The Canterbury Tales*, General Prologue: 1. 18, in *The Riverside Chaucer*, ed. L. D. Benson (3rd ed., Oxford, 1987), 23. For a modern translation, see Geoffrey Chaucer, *The Canterbury Tales*, trans. Nevill Coghill, Penguin (Harmondsworth, 1951), 19.
4. The two fourteenth-century accounts are: *Burchard of Mount Sion*, trans. Aubrey Stewart, Palestine Pilgrims' Text Society, vol. 12 (London, 1896); Henry Earl of Derby, *Expeditions to Prussia and the Holy Land, 1392*, ed. Lucy Toulmin Smith, Camden Society, n.s. 52 (London, 1894). The fifteenth-century pilgrims, apart from Margery herself in 1414, include: Nompar de Caumont (1417), Gilbert de Lannoy (1421), Bertrandon de La Brocquière (c. 1430), Bishop Louis de Rochechouart (1461), William Wey (1458 and 1462), Felix Fabri (1480 and 1483), an anonymous pilgrim from Paris (1480), Santo Brasca (1480), Bernhard von Breydenbach (1483), Paul Walther (1483), Pietro Casola (1494), and Arnold von Harff (1496–9). The editions of all their accounts are listed in *Jerusalem Journey* (see below), 219–20; also in Jonathan Sumption, *Pilgrimage: An Image of Medieval Religion* (London, 1975), 355–78.
5. Hilda F. M. Prescott, *Jerusalem Journey* (London, 1954). [An earlier version was published as *Friar Felix at Large* (New Haven, 1950).] For the rest of Felix Fabri's journey see her *Once to Sinai: The further pilgrimage of Felix Fabri* (London, 1957).
6. *The Itineraries of William Wey*, Roxburghe Club 75 (London, 1857), iii-iv.
7. William Wey, *Itineraries*, 25.
8. Ibid., 82–152.
9. Ibid., 145.
10. Ibid., 153 ff.
11. Ibid., 7 and 49.
12. Ibid., 44 and 77: 'Pinnaculum sancti sepulchri est rotundum

et factum ad modum columbaris.' This rotunda was destroyed by a fire in 1808, and the modern replacement is not of the same design.

13. For the Latin text, see Felix Fabri, *Evagatorium in Terrae Sanctae, Arabiae et Egypti Peregrinationem,* ed. C. D. Hassler, 3 vols (Stuttgart, 1843). For an English translation, see *Felix Fabri (c. 1480–1483 A.D.),* trans. Aubrey Stewart, Palestine Pilgrims' Text Society, 2 vols London, 1892), I, 207–320 and II, 321 ff.

14. Felix, *Evagatorium,* English translation, I, 208–10.

15. Felix, *Evagatorium,* Latin text: at the Holy Sepulchre, I, 238–9; at Mount Calvary, I, 298–9. Cf. English translation: I, 283 ff.; II, 364.

16. Hope Phyllis Weissman, 'Margery Kempe in Jerusalem: *Hysterica Compassio* in the Late Middle Ages', in M. J. Carruthers and E. D. Kirk, eds, *Acts of Interpretation* (Norman, Oklahoma, 1982), 201–17. The quotation is from Robert Manning of Brunne: 'She went out of her mind/ She swooned, she pined, she grew half dead,/ She fell to the ground, and beat her head.'

CHAPTER SIX

1. E. F. Jacob, *The Fifteenth Century,* Oxford History of England (Oxford, 1961), 129.

2. The account of the Lollard movement in this chapter is taken from the standard historical works on Lollardy as a political movement (as against the more recent works of scholarship on Lollard thought): K. B. MacFarlane, *John Wycliffe and the beginnings of English Nonconformity* (London, 1952; new ed., London, 1972), chs 5–6; John A. F. Thomson, *The Later Lollards, 1414–1520* (Oxford, 1965), 2–14; E. F. Jacob, *The Fifteenth Century,* Oxford History of England (Oxford, 1961), 129–33, 146–7. For Wycliffite thought, see: Edwin Robertson, *John Wycliffe: morning star of the Reformation* (Basingstoke, 1984); Anne Hudson and Pamela Gradon, eds, *English Wycliffite Sermons,* 4 vols. (Oxford, 1983–); Anne Hudson, *Lollards and their Books*

(London, 1985); Margaret Aston, *Lollards and Reformers: images and literacy in late medieval religion* (London, 1984).

3. Windeatt, 317; Meech and Allen, 308.
4. Windeatt, 318, suggests this was 10 June 1417.
5. See, for example, Meech and Allen, 314; Windeatt, 319. For a description of various lay movements of the period, found on the Continent and possibly in England, see Wolfgang Riehle, *The Middle English Mystics*, trans. Bernard Standring (London, 1981), ch. 1.

CHAPTER SEVEN

1. Hilton, *Ladder of Perfection*, 40 (Book I, ch. 36).
2. See 'Méditation', *Dictionnaire de Spiritualité*, vol. 10 (Paris, 1980), col. 906–34, particularly medieval sections, 911–19.
3. *The Spiritual Exercises of St Ignatius of Loyola*, trans. with a commentary by W. H. Longridge (London, rev. ed., 1930), 85.
4. Richard Beadle, ed., *The York Plays* (London, 1982), 323–33; also Peter Happé, ed., *English Mystery Plays*, Penguin English Library (Harmondsworth, 1975), 525–36.
5. *Meditationes Vitae Christi* [Latin text], ed. Sr M. Jordan Stallings (Washington, D.C., 1965), 106–107 (scourging); 111–13 (crucifixion). The awareness in this work that these meditations are encouraging a human use of the imagination, and are not purporting to be revelations of what actually happened in the life of Christ, is shown particularly clearly in the crucifixion scene, where the reader is offered two ways of visualising the event, whichever most pleases ('magis placet') the mind: in the first, Christ has to climb a ladder in order to be nailed to an upright cross; in the second, he is nailed to a cross laid on the ground, which is then raised and dropped into a socket. A Middle English version of this text circulated in the fifteenth century: *The mirrour of the blessed lyf of Jesu Christ*, translated by Nicholas Love, Carthusian Prior of Mount Grace (where Margery's *Book* was kept and annotated), ed. James

Hogg and Lawrence Powell, Analecta Cartusiana 91 (Salzburg, 1989).

6. For the life of St Bridget, see Helen Redpath, *God's Ambassadress: St Bridget of Sweden* (Milwaukee, 1947). For the journey to the Holy Land (12 March – 8 September 1371), see 128–33, where Bridget has a vision of the crucifixion and sobs uncontrollably, very like Margery.

7. For a Middle English version of Bridget's book, dating from the early fifteenth century, see Roger Ellis, ed., *The Liber Celestis of St Bridget of Sweden*, Early English Text Society 291 (Oxford, 1987). Bridget's account of the scourging is itself quite gory. One can see a line of development from the *Meditationes Vitae Christi*, where the emphasis is on Christ's blood pouring to the ground (see reference, n. 5 above), to Bridget (*Libar Celestis*, Bk I, ch. 10, 20), where there is no whole place left on his body to scourge, to Margery (chs 79–80).

8. John Ayton and Alexandra Barrett, eds, *Aelred of Rievaulx's De Institutione Inclusarum*, Early English Text Society 287 (Oxford, 1984), xi.

9. Aelred, *De Institutione*, ch. 14, 17–22; cf. Atkinson, *Mystic and Pilgrim*, 134–7.

10. Ignatius, *Exercises*, 91; for a more recent translation, see *Saint Ignatius of Loyola: Personal Writings*, trans. J. A. Munitiz and P. Endean, Penguin Classics (London, 1996), 306.

11. Anthony de Mello, *Sadhana: A Way to God* (Poona, 1978; New York, 1984), 88.

CHAPTER EIGHT

1. Cholmeley, *Margery Kempe*, 101.

2. Meech and Allen, xxxviii.

3. See 'Paroles intérieures', *Dictionnaire de Spiritualité*, vol. 12 (1), col. 252–7.

4. St Teresa of Avila, *The Interior Castle*, [trans. Benedictines of Stanbrook, revd. Benedict Zimmerman], Fount Classics (London, 1995) Bk 6, ch. 3, 106–22.

5. St John of the Cross, *The Ascent of Mount Carmel*, Bk 2, chs 28–31, in *The Collected Works of St John of the Cross*, trans. K. Kavanaugh and O. Rodriguez (Washington, D.C., 1991), 255–64.

6. *Dictionnaire de Spiritualité*, vol. 12 (1), col. 257. Cf. as modern examples, Benigna Consolata Ferrero, a nun (d. 1916), *Dictionnaire de Spiritualité*, vol. 5; Josepha Menendez, also a nun (d. 1923), *Dictionnaire de Spiritualité*, vol. 10.

7. St John of the Cross, *The Ascent of Mount Carmel*, Bk 2, ch. 10 (4), ch. 25 (3), ch. 27, pp. 179, 245, 252–5.

8. This hermit, a fourteenth-century Benedictine monk of either York or Durham, lived on the Inner Farne island off the coast of Northumberland. For his writings, see Hugh Farmer, ed., *The Monk of Farne*, trans. a Benedictine of Stanbrook (London, 1961).

9. The clearest example of Julian's careful making of distinctions comes in her parable of the Lord and the Servant, which does not belong to her original sequence of sixteen visions. Even here, she distinguishes what she sees 'in bodily likeness', what she receives through 'spiritual understanding', and the long drawn-out process of 'inward learning'. For the Middle English text, see *A Book of Showings to the Anchoress Julian of Norwich*, ed. E. Colledge and James Walsh, 2 vols. (Toronto, 1978), II (Long Text), chs. 50–51, pp. 510–45; for a modern translation, see Julian of Norwich, *Showings*, trans. E, Colledge and James Walsh, Classics of Western Spirituality (New York and Toronto, 1978), 265–78.

10. Latin text, *Sarum Missal*, ed. Wickham Legg, 112–13; for a text with facing English translation, *Holy Week Manual* (London, 1955), 132–4.

11. *Saint Ignatius of Loyola: Personal Writings*, trans. J. A. Munitiz and P. Endean, Penguin Classics (London, 1996), 296.

12. See *The Prayers and Meditations of St Anselm*, trans. Sr Benedicta Ward, SLG, Penguin Classics (Harmondsworth, 1973).

13. For some examples in modernised English, see *Medieval English Verse*, trans. Brian Stone, Penguin Classics (Harmondsworth, 1964; revd. ed. 1971), Nos 13, 14, 16, 17,

pp. 37–41; in Middle English, *Medieval English Lyrics,* ed. R. T. Davies (London, 1963), Nos 24, 38, 41, 46, 47, 63, 79, 102, 106, 110.

14. Thomas à Kempis, *The Imitation of Christ,* trans. Leo Sherley-Price, Penguin Classics (London, 1952), 22.

15. Thomas à Kempis, *Imitation,* 91.

16. Roger Ellis, *The Liber Celestis of St Bridget of Sweden,* ix–xii (for her Latin editors); Helen Redpath, *God's Ambassadress,* 132 (Bridget dictating in Swedish).

17. St Catherine of Siena, *The Dialogue,* trans. Suzanne Noffke, Classics of Western Spirituality (New York, 1980), 14 and 21.

18. Pepwell's *Miscellany* is reproduced in Edmund G. Gardner, *The Cell of Self-Knowledge.* For the extracts from Catherine of Siena, see pp. 35–47.

19. Roger Ellis, *The Liber Celestis of St Bridget of Sweden,* 6.

20. St Catherine of Siena, *The Dialogue,* 116–17.

21. E. I. Watkin, *Poets and Mystics,* 120.

CHAPTER NINE

1. See 'Mariage spirituel', *Dictionnaire de Spiritualité,* vol. 10, col. 388–408.

2. Raymond of Capua, *The Life of St Catherine of Siena,* trans. George Lamb (London, 1960), 99–101.

3. This literalism is not confined to Margery. See Ute Stargardt, 'The Beguines of Belgium, the Nuns of Germany and Margery Kempe', in T. J. Hefferman, ed., *The Popular Literature of Medieval England* (Knoxville, Tennessee, 1985), 277–313.

CONCLUSION

1. See, for example, St John of the Cross, *The Ascent of Mount Carmel,* Bk 2, ch. 11, 179–84.

2. St Teresa of Avila, *The Interior Castle,* Bk 7, ch. 2, 174–9.

SELECT BIBLIOGRAPHY

TEXT

British Library MS. Additional 61823.

Meech, Sandford Brown, and Allen, Hope Emily, eds, *The Book of Margery Kempe*, Early English Text Society o.s. 212 (Oxford, 1940; reprinted 1961).

TRANSLATIONS

Butler-Bowdon, William, trans., *The Book of Margery Kempe, 1436* (London: Jonathan Cape, 1936).

Triggs, Tony D., trans., *The Book of Margery Kempe: The Autobiography of the Wild Woman of God* (Tunbridge Wells, 1995).

Windeatt, Barry, trans., *The Book of Margery Kempe*, Penguin Classics (Harmondsworth, 1985).

STUDIES AND INFORMATION

Allen, Hope Emily, Letter to *The Times*, 27 December 1934.

Atkinson, Clarissa, 'In Memoriam: Hope Emily Allen (1883–1969)', *14th Century English Mystics Newsletter* [now *Mystics Quarterly*], IX (1983), 210–15.

Atkinson, Clarissa, *Mystic and Pilgrim: The Book and the World of Margery Kempe* (Ithaca and London, 1983).

Cholmeley, Katherine, *Margery Kempe: Genius and Mystic* (London, New York, Toronto, 1947).

Colledge, Edmund, *Pre-Reformation English Spirituality* (New York, 1966).

Delaney, Sheila, 'Sexual Economics, Chaucer's Wife of Bath and the *Book of Margery Kempe*', *Minnesota Review*, n.s. 5 (1975), 104–13.

Drucker, Trudy, 'The Malaise of Margery Kempe', *New York State Journal of Medicine*, 72 (1972), 2911–17.

Gallyon, Margaret, *Margery Kempe of Lynn and Medieval England* (Norwich, 1995).

Gardner, Edmund G., *The Cell of Self-Knowledge* (London and New York, 1910).

Glasscoe, Marion, *English Medieval Mystics: Games of Faith* (London and New York, 1993), ch. 6, 268–308.

Goodman, Anthony, 'The Piety of John Brunham's Daughter of Lynn', in *Medieval Women*, ed. Derek Baker (Oxford, 1978), 347–59.

Hirsch, John C., 'Author and Scribe in the *Book of Margery Kempe*', *Medium Aevum*, 44 (1975), 145–50.

Knowles, David, *The English Mystics* (London, 1927).

Knowles, David, *The English Mystical Tradition* (London, 2nd ed., 1964).

Lochrie, Karma, '*The Book of Margery Kempe*: The Marginal Woman's Quest for Literary Authority', *Journal of Medieval and Renaissance Studies*, 16 (1986), 33–55.

Medcalf, Stephen, ed., *The Later Middle Ages* (London, 1981).

Porter, Roy, *A Social History of Madness: Stories of the Insane* (London, 1987), ch. 6: 'Mad Women', 103–12.

Riehle, Wolfgang, trans. Bernard Standring, *The Middle English Mystics* (London, 1981).

Watkin, Edward I., *Poets and Mystics* (London and New York, 1953), ch. 6: 'In defense of Margery Kempe', 104–35.

Weissman, Hope Phyllis, 'Margery Kempe in Jerusalem: *Hysterica Compassio* in the Late Middle Ages', in M. J. Carruthers and E. D. Kirk, eds, *Acts of Interpretation* (Norman, Oklahoma, 1982), 201–17.